Intimacy and Midlife

Intimacy and Midlife

Understanding Your Journey
with Yourself, Others, and God

Robert J. Faucett
and
Carol Ann Faucett

CROSSROAD • NEW YORK

1990

The Crossroad Publishing Company
370 Lexington Avenue, New York, NY 10017

Printed in the United States of America
Typesetting output: TEXSource, Houston

Library of Congress Cataloging-in-Publication Data

Faucett, Robert, 1943–
    Intimacy and midlife : understanding your journey with yourself,
others, and God / Robert J. Faucett and Carol Ann Faucett.
       p. cm.
    Includes bibliographical references and index.
    ISBN 0-8245-1038-0 (pbk.)
    1. Middle aged persons—Conduct of life. 2. Middle aged persons—
Religious life. 3. Middle age—Psychological aspects.
I. Faucett, Carol Ann, 1945– . II. Title.
BJ1690.F38 1990
248.8'4—dc20   90-45493
                                                      CIP

To the community and leaders
of the Pecos Benedictine Monastery in Pecos, New Mexico,
more affectionately known simply as "Pecos."
From the seeds of their vision, wisdom, and spirituality,
this book was born.

Contents

Introduction

Americans are becoming ever more aware of the concept originally observed by Swiss psychiatrist Carl Jung that there is a major life change during the middle years. We are part of a society which *historically* rode out the storms of such life changes in ourselves and others with a hope and a prayer that life would one day return to normal. Today, however, our society waits for little. If there is a problem, we fix it. If something is amiss, we change it. If something doesn't feel good, we do what we must until it does feel good.

As a result of this attitude, Westerners, Christian and non-Christian alike, are less willing to wait out the discomforts of midlife; consequently, they frequently make dramatic changes in their lives when they encounter their midlife turbulence. Part of the problem we face is that these changes are frequently inappropriate and often have a disastrous effect on our lives and those around us. If the inappropriate changes are not of our own doing, then others such as our friends, family, boss, spouse, pastor, or children are experiencing midlife and making changes that have a dramatic effect on our lives.

Our way as Christians is often severely shaken during these times. Our own belief systems can come undone. What seemed to be clearly right or wrong our entire life no longer seems quite as clear. Fantasies we thought we had put behind us when we were eighteen suddenly resurface and we feel bewildered, out of control, and embarrassed.

Whether or not we are Christians, these changes in ourselves and others can and do cause a great deal of pain. We find ourselves bewildered and asking deep questions about what is going on. What is expected of us? Are there constructive changes we can make?

Our own experience is that putting this midlife process in an understandable structure can go a long way toward helping us to understand what is happening to us and those around us. By better understanding these seeming illogical changes and phases of life, we can often begin to settle down and allow some of them to happen without the panic and often damaging false starts we can make in an attempt to *fix our problem.*

That is the purpose of this book: to present in an understandable and useful form the changes we are apt to experience at midlife and in so doing to give understanding and, more importantly, *authority* to our experience. When we receive authority, we can begin to trust that we are not going crazy; that we are normal; that we are not a bad Christian because we are experiencing these dilemmas.

The changes we experience at midlife are not only normal, they are *necessary* if we are to fully live our second half of life with the blessings and freedom which God seems to desire for us. The sense of uncertainty, loss, and fear that accompany this midlife experience is a valuable process which will greatly enrich the second half of our life.

We believe midlife is an invitation to *intimacy*, intimacy in a much different sense than we discovered when we were twenty and falling in love. Intimacy perhaps in a different sense than we believe it to mean today. The intimacy of which we speak is, first, an intimacy with *ourselves* as we begin to understand parts of ourselves we have hidden for forty or fifty years. Intimacy with *others* as we allow ourselves to really know another person and be known by another person, be it our spouse, family, community member, or friend. Intimacy which comes from a quiet commitment to lay down our life for another.

Finally, this midlife involves an invitation to intimacy with *God* as he calls us to himself in this second half of life. This intimacy comes from really *knowing his will* for us at the very core of who we are. Really knowing that we are loved and that we have the potential to move into our second half of life living not according to what others will think, but according to what God wants of us as his Child.

During the past years, we have set out to better understand

this awesome creature God has created known as the human being. The human sciences have shed great light on this understanding, but unfortunately such insights are often presented in an agnostic or even atheistic framework which makes much of the information difficult to comprehend for Christians, let alone integrate and make useful.

We offer this subject of midlife not as psychologists but as qualified lay Christians who have endeavored to make use of the subject in our own lives and ministry. We are both well versed in understanding human behavior and have led workshops throughout the world. Our previous book was a study of Christian personality.[1]

We have been married twenty-six years and have two grown children. Bob was an executive with the Bell System for twenty years and together we now operate Look Beyond Ministries, our full-time vocation through which we offer parish missions, retreats, and workshops.

Over the past fourteen years we have been extensively involved in various forms of lay ministry. After a long absence, our church involvement began following a Marriage Encounter Weekend and introduction to a fully alive parish in 1976. We have extensive training and experience in youth ministry, family ministry, marriage preparation, and parish leadership. We have held various positions in our diocese of Metuchen, New Jersey. Bob was the head of the Evangelization Commission and served on the Bishop's Pastoral Council and Commission of Ecumenical and Interreligious Affairs.

Look Beyond Ministries was formed in 1978 from our home which served as a center offering retreats for families and young people, days of recollection, Christian concerts, workshops, and other events. During that time we coordinated and developed most of those programs along with others in our local community.

We offer our ministry throughout the United States, functioning with the approval of our bishop, Edward Hughes.[2] In 1984 Bob resigned from AT&T and Look Beyond Ministries became our full-time vocation. Since then we have traveled extensively offering retreat and parish missions on the topics of prayer, family, personality, and midlife. We have led numerous workshops for church leaders and religious communities using the subject of this and our previous book.

The focus of our first book was the human personality including specific gifts which were identified by Carl Jung and further developed by Isabel Briggs Myers and the Myers-Briggs Type Indicator. Given a Christian application, our thesis is that we are called to a spiritual freedom in using all of the gifts God has given to us as human beings, including, but not limited to, our strengths. As we move on and grow in life, we are called to develop gifts that are latent during the first half of our life but which begin to come to the fore during the time known as midlife.

Within the context of our book and Christian workshops we began to elaborate on the concept of midlife and discovered two things. First, a great deal of the readers of our book and participants in our workshops were in some sort of midlife transition themselves. Second, when we asked participants to name the topic about which they desired more information, they consistently identified the subject of midlife. From these observations came our very fruitful workshops on midlife and the present book.

It was our prayer as we wrote this book that whoever read it would be drawn to the freedom and intimacy God so desires for us all.

1

The Rhythm of Midlife

Take off your sandals for the place where you are standing is holy ground.
—Exodus 3:5

Crisis, divorce, infidelity, doubt, catastrophe, failure, or uncertainty. Words we hear connected with midlife sometimes deter us from further exploration. They may make us wonder why we should bother giving attention to such a painful life episode. Perhaps if we ignore it, it won't bother us; maybe it will just "go away." We have all heard many times, "I don't have *time* for midlife!" This really means "I refuse to make time for such a painful experience."

Our modern culture views midlife as a horrid time in one's life. We may often avoid reading, listening to, or entering into conversations about midlife because we have such a negative understanding of what it will mean for us. In this book, we do not offer a painless view of midlife, but we do offer a view with hope.

RHYTHMS

Understanding the pattern and rhythm of midlife can be of tremendous value. Each person will find his or her unique pattern but will also share similarities with others. Periodically we must move forward, sometimes backward, and yet occasionally, by necessity, we stand still.

Midlife is a time of passage from one stage of life to another. It takes us from the first half of life, filled with its outward focus, establishing our identity and making our mark in the world, to the second half of life with its inward focus and increasing mellowness. For some this evolution will come about somewhat smoothly; for others it will be experienced with considerable pain and uncertainty. Each will experience this crossroads of life in an understandably unique manner.

While midlife is a time of uncertainty and doubt for many of us, these years can bring us much growth, hope, and cause for celebration. It can be a time when we experience a sense of newness of life and a freedom we never may have known before. The rhythm of midlife, like the ebb and flow of the tide, can overpower us with doubts and uncertainty, yet it has the potential to bring us to a new place in life, to a new vantage point where we can explore our full potential as a Child of God.

HOLY GROUND

This stage of our growth brings with it the capacity for the believer to experience a new presence of God. We are given the rare opportunity to examine our lives and possibly reorientate ourselves and the way we will live out the remainder of life.

God was present to Moses on Mount Horeb and spoke to him through the burning bush (Exodus 3:1–6). At midlife we may sometimes experience a sense of being much like that burning bush: ablaze, uncomfortable, unsettled. We may question ourselves and God. We may ask what our lives are all about. Yet God is deeply present in the midlife experience. He is present to us as he was to Moses in the burning bush. The Lord is speaking to us saying, "I am with you in your uncertainty and trials. I am with you in your burning bush experience. Take off your sandals for the place where you are standing is holy ground."

The transformations of midlife invite us into a deeper intimacy with the Father, Son, and Holy Spirit. The midlife process itself is also a call to intimacy with ourselves and others with whom we share this life. In this stage of transition we will experience change, and change by its very nature may not always be comfortable or pleasant, but it is indeed a time for us to let go and let God take more and more control of our lives. We urge you as you read this book and make this journey to reverence this time of your life; it is a holy time; you are standing on Holy Ground.

THE CHANGE OF MIDLIFE

We do not initiate midlife; rather, it happens to us. At times, outside circumstances may trigger the transition. Events such as an uninitiated divorce or separation, the death of a close friend or family member, the personal injury or illness of yourself or someone close may bring on the transition. For others it may be a change of financial status, or loss or change of a job that may bring about the change of midlife. A son or daughter leaving home may trigger an inner reaction of uncertainty and questioning. Even seemingly good things like a new home, retirement, or a job promotion can elicit our midlife challenge. The same event that leads one person into the crossroads of midlife may have little effect on another.

Change and transition do not come naturally to anyone, nor would we usually choose painful change if we had a choice. We are naturally resistant to changing things in our lives, including career, lifestyle, or our place of residence. Even with good changes, we may experience a degree of loss. A seeming positive change such as a job promotion carries some strain. We often lose comfortable relationships. We may have fears about our ability to perform the new responsibilities and our ability to meet others' expectations. We may feel a sense of loss about our old position which may have fit like an "old shoe." When transition is inevitable, we sometimes feel uprooted and shaken by the outer events as well as the inner uncertainty that frequently accompanies the change.

PATTERNS OF CHANGE

We need to look at our response to this time of midlife. We can learn much about our own response by reflecting upon our pattern or rhythm of dealing with changes in the past. How do we historically approach our transitions? Do we do so with a sense of wonder or of fear? With an attitude of anticipation or of clinging to the past? Do we tend to act passively or actively when it comes to change? The style we have developed for dealing with change is the product both of early influences in childhood and of our later life.

What sort of attitude do we need to develop which will help us to respond to this rhythm of midlife? As we look at change in ourselves, we discover that midlife can truly become a time of reverence during which we honor the creation God has made of us and this time of *holy transition.*

LEARNING FROM OTHERS' MIDLIFE

How have others responded to the transition of midlife? By reflecting upon some of the people who have gone before us we can notice how others managed to grow through this time of midlife. Let us take, for example, the life of St. Ignatius of Loyola. In his early thirties as a soldier he suffered a leg wound in a war. The following seventeen years of his life were years of deep emotional uncertainty. It was a time of loneliness and searching for new goals. During these years Ignatius experienced his religious conversion and significant spiritual growth. It was during this time that he wrote what is now known as the Spiritual Exercises of St. Ignatius, a retreat experience of prayer and discernment that is still experienced by many to this day. For Ignatius, like many others, midlife was a time of deep and life-changing spiritual enlightenment which benefited many.

Mother Teresa of Calcutta provides us with another example of transition as we reflect upon her call to a change of direction at midlife. At the age of thirty-six she felt a call to give up her work at the Bengal missions, where she had been very happy, and begin her ministry with the poorest of the poor in Calcutta. Her response to God's call at midlife encouraged many others to share this kind of love in action to relieve human misery.

There are also many others such as Carl Jung himself, St. Augustine, and St. Elizabeth Ann Seton, who are examples of successful change and reorientation at midlife.

We can look at St. Paul's experience of conversion and see a pattern of midlife transition. He was a Jewish activist in the midst of a zealous religious career when he suffered a breakdown. He experienced confusion and disorientation (Acts 9:1–22). He was blinded by a light, fell to the ground, and Jesus spoke to him. Among the Christian community at Damascus his eyesight was restored and he saw differently, with a reorientation that led to a radically different career and life.

Jesus Christ shows us by his life, passion, death, and resurrection how we, too, as Christians can move through the midlife transition. "Unless a grain of wheat falls into the earth and dies, it remains alone, but if it dies, it bears much fruit" (John 12:24).

Midlife requires a death to what has been and an acceptance of the new life yet unseen. There is ambiguity, uncertainty and moments of doubt and disorientation, yet God is with us.

As one woman described herself at midlife, "I have come to a point in my life where I am not willing to continue living in the same manner. My relationship with my husband is of utmost importance to me, as well as my continued relationship with my grown children. Yet deep inside of me I know there is a part of me that has not yet really lived, a part of me that longs for expression, and nurturing. It needs fertile soil, and care to allow this seed of new life to begin to grow and bloom. What exactly does this mean? I'm not sure, but I know I have to discover what that means for me personally. I will do that through trial and error, through some exploration and study of new areas of interest. It is not all that clear, but I know I have to search, to follow that quiet, still voice within me and with time and patience I believe this new life will evolve."

This woman's heartfelt search is shared by many women at midlife. For many, it is a clear calling, to go to college, to attain a graduate degree, to seek new careers. For others it is impossible to articulate even as it begins to resolve itself, but the inner search, the questions, need to be asked. The journey needs to be taken and explored.

MIDLIFE SUPPORT GROUPS

As we lead our workshops and retreats throughout the country on this subject and talk about the rhythm of midlife in our own lives and those of others, we find people are often relieved to know they are not alone in their turmoil and uncertainties. Most helpful at this stage can be a support group of individuals or couples who are all experiencing the transition of midlife. The ability to share and verbalize about this time of life and pray together can be extremely valuable. A support group can both encourage its members and create an atmosphere of trust and listening as well as a time of prayer to call upon the Lord for help and the grace to see us through this often difficult experience.

We may find, as we meet with others, that the most difficult yet important quality we can cultivate at midlife is to listen to one another. In such a group we are not called to have all the answers, nor to solve everyone's problems, nor to look down on others as wrong, but to be a person who will listen, care, empathize, and understand. Responding with understanding helps others to reveal themselves more deeply. Being listened to helps us through the uncertainty of midlife. Blessed by such a group for over a year, we met with six couples from our own parish twice monthly to share, discuss, and pray about our activities specifically focused on the subject of midlife. During this time together the couples were challenged to look inside, at themselves and at their relationships with one another. Sometimes, we shared things wondering, "Will anyone understand?" Only then did we find there were others in the group who had a similar situation or experience. We were not alone and we could name those experiences that were a natural part of this time of transition.

Some found a deeper commitment and desire to communicate at a new level which required a vulnerability that they had never experienced before. Some members of the group expressed how they had talked with others about midlife topics and some of the changes they were experiencing without that kind of dark cloud of the "midlife crisis" hanging over them. Still others found that people at work were interested to find out what our topic of discussion had been the previous week. Now, some time later, everyone in the group has expressed how helpful the year had been for them individually and as a couple. It gave them both a freedom and authority to their experience. Although we have moved from the parish, the couples continue to meet regularly.

At the conclusion of several of the chapters, we have included many of the useful sharing and discussion questions used during this year as well as those we use in our workshops. We have also recorded a reasonably priced six-part video series on this subject designed mainly to be used by groups in homes, parishes, and retreat centers.[1] We strongly urge that the element of prayer be a constant and prolonged part of all such groups. In our own group we made it a practice to open with a time of prayer, intercession, and song, and one of the couples would prepare a closing prayer experience each session as well.

With the help of others, and with God's grace, we can begin to understand and move through these changes gradually and with a renewed hope and strength from this very spiritual experience called midlife.

OUR OWN MIDLIFE TRANSITIONS — CAROL ANN

As I, Carol Ann, reflect on the beginning of my own midlife transition, I recall the trigger of one of many changes in my life. At the time I was thirty-eight years old. (At this writing, I am forty-four). My life was progressing rather well. I was faithful to my time of prayer, to the sacramental life, and to the call of service to others. At the same time I was experiencing an uneasiness with a friendship. In my own estimation things were not going well between myself and a good friend. I experienced a strong inner tension and turmoil. I remember praying regularly asking the Lord to mend this relationship; to give me a way to work through my many uncertainties. While attending a week-long retreat, I heard a song that struck me to the core, and I was moved to tears by one of its lines: "I'm not going to move the mountain, but I'm going to teach you to climb." I had been asking the Lord to make things better in my relationship. Instead I sensed he was calling me to climb the mountain and I knew it would not be an easy ascent. I felt a call to growth, a challenge to take some difficult steps on the natural level I would rather not have taken.

I ended the relationship. It was neither comfortable nor easy to do. I didn't deal well with conflict at the time but I believed it was the right thing to do, however difficult and painful. I believed God would give me the grace to carry me through this time. As I look back now, I know he did indeed teach me to "climb the mountain."

This was the beginning of my midlife transition. It was a time of growth, change, and pain. At times I felt as if my world was falling apart around me. I experienced times of inward struggle and a letting go of the past to embrace something new. At times I felt down; at other times I experienced a freedom to develop my God-given gifts and talents. It was truly a turning point in my life. It was the beginning of understanding myself better, my motivations and my reasons for certain behavior patterns. This midlife change was the threshold to a new depth in my relationship with God. This was a major turning point that is ever evolving, stirring me to intimacy in relationship with myself, God, and others. I feel as if I am just beginning to learn and live the fullness of life God desires for me.

Since that time I have experienced many other facets of my midlife change. Two grown children leaving home has invited me to let go of them in a concrete way. Our ministry, known as Look Beyond Ministries, became a full-time venture for Bob and me after he ended his career with the telephone company and I ended my own career as housewife and community volunteer. These changes have initiated a challenge for growth in our own marriage relationship and our communications. We are working together as well as living and loving together. It has been an adjustment for us both as well as a deepening of our love and commitment to one another. This new life has challenged me to grow and to learn, to reach deep inside and believe in some God-given gifts I had put aside. These changes have not come easily. At times I've felt as if I've been caught in the middle of a storm that was going on inside as well as outside of me. I know that I have more areas of transition and change ahead of me. I don't know for certain what lies ahead. I feel a renewed sense of hope about myself and my life. I believe that with God's help and grace he will see me through these middle years of change.

OUR OWN MIDLIFE TRANSITIONS — BOB

For me, Bob, midlife seemed to begin at about the age of thirty-nine. (At this writing, I am forty-five). I had completed seventeen very successful years as an executive with the Bell System. I had worked my way up the corporate ladder and was considered a "fast track" executive. Suddenly, I couldn't get an assignment that "worked." The telephone industry was amidst a great upheaval as court cases were pending and uncertainty about our job and company became the only certainty. Like so many others in the corporate world, rather than wondering what job would lie ahead, we began to wonder if any job was ahead.

I was assigned organizations to head which would suddenly disappear from organization charts, or responsibilities would suddenly vanish when reorganizations would vaporize entire operations. People for whom I was responsible came to me for answers which I couldn't give and I had serious concerns about myself.

Finally, in 1983 a federal judge ruled the Bell System was to be broken up, and the little stability remaining was dissolved. A historic telephone industry event known as divestiture turned many lifelong careers upside down, including my own. I took an assignment with our parent company, AT&T, with a temporary role of helping to manage the breakup of the company and supervise this traumatic experience for several states in the Midwest. I saw people uprooted, rejected, discouraged, and clamoring for position in the evolving structures. People like myself who had made dramatic, permanent career choices suddenly regretted their choices and could not recover.

The company was overstaffed and after a year began to devise economic plans to "down size" (the wonderful corporate term for firing people) staff. In retrospect, I give credit to those who designed such programs to have them remain voluntary.

Just before the second offer of a year's pay in return for a resignation, I began to sense that a part of my life had ended. I had joined the telephone company when I was twenty-two years old, just before our youngest child was born, and I loved it. It had provided a wonderful, rewarding career but now it was ending. I knew it would never be the same, and I felt sad to see so many people, whom I had grown to love and respect, spread over a diversity of competing organizations quite dissimilar to the phone company they had signed on with in their younger days. I was going to miss the "old days" and that hurt a bit. I found myself losing the vigor to start my days at work which I had had for so many years.

But then, a vision Carol Ann and I had some six years earlier began to clarify. We had bought a large unfinished home as an investment. While we were finishing it, it became somewhat of a retreat center, hosting Christian concerts, family and youth retreats, and days of recollection. When we originally bought the house, we envisioned one day selling it when it was finished and using the profit to begin full-time ministry.

After six years the house was finished, and we began to pray, plan, and discern. The following year I ended my twenty-year career and accepted the company's departure offer. We sold our home, built a much smaller one and began our ministry on a full-time basis and it continues to evolve.

While this all sounds somewhat simple, the process was not without a great deal of pain, uncertainty, and false starts. One of the most painful was to let go of the image of myself I had built over seventeen years of hard and satisfying work.

By no means do we feel like our own midlife transition is complete at forty-four and forty-five. Even as we write, we are in the midst of further change as we have sold our home again and built another in northeastern Pennsylvania. Rather, we feel as if we are *in* midlife. Much has been accomplished yet much more lies ahead. The grace we feel now is an awareness of the rhythm, the ebb and flow of midlife. We look forward to the future with anticipation and excitement, knowing the rhythm goes on. As we continue explaining the process of midlife, we will share more of our stories as it is appropriate. We hope our readers will find them helpful.

2

Stages of Life

The most common question we are asked about midlife is "Exactly *when* is midlife?" Our tongue-in-cheek response is, "First, the 'good' news. Midlife is somewhere between thirty-five and sixty. The 'bad news' is that for some of us midlife is the *entire time* between thirty-five and sixty! In reality, the amount of time midlife lasts is different for each person, but generally it will unfold and last for several years.

There are many theories regarding the human psychological life cycle and the different stages of growth experienced throughout our life from our moment of conception to our death. For the purpose of this book, we will focus on the specific transition at midlife. Jung called the movement into the second half of life a "psychic birth." The first half of life is for the development of the ego or the outer personality, while the second half of life is for the fuller development of the *total* personality. In the second half of life we are called to center our lives around an emerging set of values and criteria. As we redirect energies formerly used for *external* adaptation toward fostering *inner* growth, the essential task of the midlife transition can begin to flow.

MIDLIFE IS TRANSITION

It is important to remember that midlife is a *transition*. A life transition moves us from one stage of life to another. Midlife is the transition from the first half of our life to the second

11

half of our life. The fact is, we live our lives much differently during the first half of life as compared to the second half of life.

STAGES OF LIFE

First Half of Life	Second Half of Life
Outward Focus	Inward Focus
Establish Identity	Striving to Balance
Career Choices	Spiritual and Personal Growth
State and Style of Life Choices	Discover Value of Crosses
Intimacy with Others — Family, Community, etc.	Forgiveness of Self and Others
Conquer the World	Authentic Identity
Sunrise Perspective	Sunset Perspective

THE FIRST HALF OF LIFE

The first half of life is a time of more outward focus during which we expend a great deal of energy in an attempt to establish our outward identity. We ask: "Who am I?" "How do I desire others to view me?" We make our mark in the world, we climb the ladder of success, make our career choices, and desire to get ahead and reach certain goals. We choose the style and state of life in which we will live. We decide if we will marry and have children, remain single, or perhaps enter religious life. It is usually the time we decide where we will reside and purchase our first home. The first half of life is a time in which we move toward intimacy with others as we choose a life mate and/or develop meaningful relationships with others. Our focus in the first half of our lives is accentuated by the outer world concentration. It is a time of ego development, of doing and achieving.

It is essential that we develop these characteristics and achieve these tasks in the first half of our life. They are critical to our overall growth and development and should not be short-circuited. It is beneficial to the entire life cycle to develop and give these characteristics of life the full attention they deserve in order to move through the transitions of the remainder of our life.

Failure to live our first half of life accomplishing its rightful tasks can have much the same effect of premature movement into any new life phase. Children forced into adulthood before they can develop their childhood fully can stifle their adult development. We may know of young children who were forced into parent roles vis-à-vis their younger siblings. They may have a difficult time later on in life when their stunted need for a healthy childhood surfaces.

Likewise, one who does not do the work of life's first half during its allotted time may have a difficult second half. Years ago we had a friend who was coerced into working in the family business right out of college. While he was named president of the firm, a domineering father continued to make key decisions and treat him as a child. At midlife, he experienced a renewed desire to strike out on his own and take control of his life. Though his father now lived far away, he would not allow his grown son the independence he required, and the son began a competing firm in an effort to finally make his own mark.

Likewise, many women who during their first half of life were required to put their own identity aside to take on the roles of wife and mother may need to strike out on their own later in order to belatedly accomplish the goal of their first half. We will speak more of this common experience in later chapters.

Sunrise Perspective

During the first half of our lives, we see life in the time perspective of *now* back to the beginning when we were born. We often think of ourselves as eternally young, perhaps as a teen. Part of this outlook involves a sense of immortality. We cannot imagine ourselves dying. Here we see one of the reasons we did such dangerous things when we were young and why our children still do them. They simply believe they are not going to die! They are invincible just as we believed ourselves to be at their age. We may have had some experiences in our lives we would never share with our kids today for fear they might go out and do them. (Sometimes we would rather not hear what they do today either!) Yet no matter how dangerous, all of this is part of the sunrise perspective that seems to be inherent within each of us during the first half of our lives.

Jung uses the wonderful analogy of the sun to describe this first half outlook. He says,

I must take for comparison the daily course of the sun. . . . In the morning it rises from the nocturnal sea of consciousness and looks upon the wide, bright world which lies before it in an expanse that steadily widens the higher it climbs in the firmament. In this extension of its field of action caused by its own rising, the sun will discover its significance; it will see the attainment of the greatest possible height, and the widest possible dissemination of its blessings, as its goal. In this conviction the sun pursues its course to the unforeseen zenith — unforeseen, because its career is unique and individual, and the culminating point could not be calculated in advance.[1]

Here Jung gives credence to our ever widening outlook toward the world. As we move toward midlife, we discover how much broader and expansive is the world than we first believed.

THE SECOND HALF OF LIFE

The second half of our lives are lived much differently than the first. Here we are invited to a focus which is more inward. Augustine exhorts us, "Enter into yourself; it is in the interior man [or woman], where truth is found." The inward focus consists of better understanding ourselves and our motivations. We may begin to ask, "Why do we behave as we do?" "Who are we in *God's eyes?*" "What is our purpose in life?"

This inward focus is meant to give us an understanding of how God has made us and in turn to help us to love and treat others in a more Christian way. It is not, however, intended to leave us self-centered. Rather, it seems to be designed as a vehicle to help us understand our motivations so we might be more faithful in the commandment of loving ourselves, God, and neighbor. Our potential for intimacy with ourselves, others, and God can increase tremendously as we work through these invitations to grow at midlife.

This intimacy at midlife is much different than the intimacy of the first half of our life. There is an opportunity for new depth and meaning to the word "intimacy" as we grow and discern through the many experiences life will bring to us. Intimacy in terms of life's second half deals less with a physical, romantic and even psychological closeness than with a "spiritual" intimacy, be it with God, ourselves or another person.

"Be still and know that I am God" (Psalm 46:10). It is sometimes difficult in our hectic, fast-paced society to have this inner focus. We are exhorted to get out and accomplish and gather everything we can on the way.

Jesus tells us, "The kingdom of God is within you" (Luke 17:20). The second half of life is ultimately a call to attain a spiritual reorientation to life, a rebirth.

Generativity

Another psychologist, Erick Erickson, focused his theories around certain *crisis* times as a person moves through life. Each particular crisis revolves around a specific human task. For example, Erickson describes the latter years of a person's development in terms of the human task of "generativity." Generativity, connected with the words *generate* and *generation*, involves using our gifts in the *service* of the Kingdom and future generations of humanity. This sometimes involves efforts expended in which we might not see the fruits of our work in our own lifetime. Generativity sometimes involves handing on the faith to others by mature leadership that enables and empowers them to use their gifts for the community and the world. The opposite of generativity would be stagnation or continuing to function in a first-half mode of "accomplishing" and "identity creation" for our own sake. Failure to respond to this call can render us passive, dormant, and stagnant in our personal as well as religious lives.

Our life pattern is a journey of growth from birth to death. Common patterns are found in nearly all psychological theories of midlife. No two people are exactly alike and our individual response to midlife will be unique. Nevertheless, midlife is a time of potential growth and change, a turning point in our life cycle.

Balance

As we move into the second half of life, there should naturally be a striving for more of a *balance* in life. We are invited to live our life with more of a stance of open hands. To allow life to happen, to go with the flow instead of constantly trying to fight the current. This does not mean we fail to take responsibility and act on our life, but we are called to use the old axiom "Let go and let God."

We strive to find a balance of harmony in our inner and outer lives. We may be active and involved but we are also taking time just to be. We may find that we desire to come to an equilibrium when it comes to our possessions and a simplification of our life. We may come to terms by seeing the difference between our wants and our needs. This balance can also show forth in a new discovery of our gifts as well as our limitations.

Spiritual and Personal Growth

The second half of our lives is a time for spiritual and personal growth. Here we find a reward of our newly developing inward focus. Life's second half brings with it a quiet yet consistent inner call to conversion and a fundamental renewal of body, mind, and spirit. Even if during the first half of our life we have known God in a personal way and lived a deeply pious and spiritual life, during our second half we are invited to deepen this intimacy as we change and mature through this wonderful passage of life. We will speak much more of this in future chapters.

Individuation

Our second half of life is a time of *individuation*. Individuation is a term employed by Jung which describes a process through which we discover our unique potential and personal path in life; as such, it is found in discovering God's Will for us. Jung was the first to recognize that individuation actually occurs and is sorely needed in our second half of life and he was intimately aware of the spiritual nature of the process. Yet individuation takes a lifetime of living life faithfully and learning from our relationships and experiences and listening to God. It is toward this deeply spiritual experience that each of us in midlife is invited. It is toward this same goal that this book attempts to lead.

Discovering the Value of Our Crosses

The second half of our life is a time to discover the value of the crosses in our lives. We begin to learn from our mistakes and sufferings, to see the value of the errors we have made. Painful experiences in the first half of our life might seem meaningless until now.

I, Bob, remember when Carol Ann and I were first married

and I was trying to discover a career for myself before joining the telephone company. I started a small business which failed. At the same time, we ran up huge credit-card bills and other debts. At one point, one of us always had to be in our apartment as we feared the landlord would lock us out for nonpayment of our rent. Finally, our car was repossessed and we had to move in with my dad. During much of the years that followed, I tried to put the memories of that experience out of my mind as I considered it the low point of my life. I felt I had been a failure and was embarrassed and humiliated by the experience.

Only recently was I able to recall that experience and begin to see the value of that ordeal. As we recovered from the hardship of being broke, we paid off all of our creditors and we began to work very hard on our personal financial management. From that time on, we never used a credit card and we never borrowed money except for our mortgages. We spent money very conservatively and put all we could into our homes and savings. I realize now, as a result of learning the very painful lessons from being broke, we have the financial flexibility today to live the lifestyle we live and to minister in the way we feel called. Thus, the eighteen months I previously regarded as an embarrassing cross, I see today as a wonderful blessing.

Take Responsibility

During our second half of life we are called to take responsibility for our lives and stop blaming others for our shortcomings and weaknesses. Whatever the circumstances of our lives, we are responsible for our choices and how we live. If we were mistreated as a child, or lived with alcoholism; if our parents failed us in some way, we are now called to view these circumstances as an opportunity for growth. We need to ask, "How am I a better person because of my past?" or "How can I be an instrument of healing to others who have walked this path?" We must try to understand what good can come from this time. How was God present to us? As we pray with God's help and his grace we may see with new eyes and new compassion and understanding the crosses we have carried.

Without a doubt, this area of adult development is recently the most widely researched and written about. Programs such as Adult Children of Alcoholics and other "twelve-step programs" offer tremendous help and support to adults trying to work through childhood memories and experiences. Books dealing with co-dependency offer further resources as well.

Forgiveness

In our second half of life we will find ourselves invited to a stance of forgiveness: to let go of hurts from our past and to forgive ourselves as well as others, and perhaps even God. Lack of forgiveness is one of the major barriers to work through as we move into our postmidlife years.

Sunset Perspective

In the second half, our perspective on life will move to more of a sunset point of view. We begin to think in terms of how much time we have left and how we want to live that time here on earth. Continuing with Jung's words quoted above, he said of this second-half perspective, "At the stroke of noon the descent begins. And the descent means the reversal of all the ideals and values that were cherished in the morning. The sun falls into contradiction with itself. It is as though it should draw in its rays instead of emitting them."[2]

During the second half, we view life less in terms of the time we have been alive than in terms of our time left. We are in touch with our own mortality and we become better equipped to face our own deaths. We are able to face the sunset of our lives if we have successfully dealt with the many questions and invitations that midlife brings.

Authentic Identity

During our second half of life we are called to establish a more *authentic identity*. This more genuine identity will be drawn more from God's Will for us as opposed to what others might think about us or what we perceive is expected of us from others, our peers and parents included. During the second half of life, the identity we portray has the potential to be more accurate and faithful to our true inner self. This concept of authentic identity is the very spiritual work of individuation which will constitute much of the focus of the chapters which follow.

While all of the above are second-half-of-life patterns for growth, they are intertwined with one another. These changes may advance slowly and painstakingly, yet they will bring with them a new-found freedom in our understanding and intimacy with ourselves, others, and God.

QUESTION FOR PERSONAL REFLECTION AND SMALL-GROUP SHARING

Suggested Scripture: Ecclesiastes 3:1–8

There is a season for everything, a time for every occupation under the heaven:

> *A time for giving birth,*
> *a time for dying;*
> *a time for planting,*
> *a time for uprooting what has been planted.*
> *A time for killing,*
> *a time for healing;*
> *a time for knocking down,*
> *a time for building.*
> *A time for tears,*
> *a time for laughter;*
> *a time for mourning,*
> *a time for dancing.*
> *A time for throwing stones away,*
> *a time for gathering them up;*
> *a time for embracing,*
> *a time to refrain from embracing.*
> *A time for searching,*
> *a time for losing;*
> *a time for keeping,*
> *a time for throwing away,*
> *a time for tearing,*
> *a time for sewing;*
> *a time for keeping silent,*
> *a time for speaking.*

A time for loving,
a time for hating;
a time for war,
a time for peace.

PERSONAL REFLECTION AND PRAYER
PRELIMINARY NOTE

Begin this time of prayer by settling quietly in God's presence. Remind yourself of God's love for you. Ask for help to bring to mind the aspects of the first half of your life upon which God desires you to reflect.

REFLECTIONS FOR PRAYER

1. During the first half of life, especially in the late teens and early twenties, we begin to develop close relationships with others. When did this become important to me? How did it unfold in my life?
A. In friendships?
B. In commitment to marriage or religious life?

2. Considering the characteristics of the first half of life listed on the left of the chart on page 12, what most resonates with me? Were there specific areas that I most recall from that period of my life?

3. As life's second half comes upon me, how have I seen myself drawn to the inward focus which is so often a part? How is your relationship with God affected by this gentle call.

SMALL-GROUP-SHARING QUESTIONS

1. There are many different kinds of identities we can establish. A few are: successful business person, good wife and mother, doctor, lawyer, helpful neighbor, good provider, good father and husband, flirt, athlete, jock, cheerleader, cute, nice, mean, and so on. Recall one or two periods in the first half of your life. With what identity did you view yourself? How did you hope others would think of you?

2. When you made your career choices, were you influenced by role models? Did you want to be like others? In what way?

3. During the first half of life, did forming close relationships come easily or with difficulty? Explain.

   4. As you reflect back to the first half of your life, what characteristic from the "First Half of Life" list most stands out to you now? How do you feel about that?

3

Stages of Midlife Transition

Whenever we try to fit a complexity as multifarious as the universe or the psyche into a manageable structure we distort and simplify it. This holds true as we try to place the incredibly complex process of the midlife transition into stages. Nevertheless, with that said, there remains a value in understanding the apparent phases we are likely to encounter during midlife. However vague, we can be better equipped to anticipate and understand them when they occur. We caution the reader to view these stages with flexibility since, in reality, they are likely to be "messy." They will overlap, stretch out longer than normal, skip certain steps, and probably repeat themselves along the way. Thus, while this and other psychological structures are helpful, they must be treated with a good deal of flexibility.

By structuring and understanding the different stages of midlife, we can better recognize how these *stages* are acted out and be able to apply them on our own journey. By recognizing these stages as they arise, we have the potential to become less compulsive in the way they manifest themselves and are acted out, and perhaps we can behave in a less erratic fashion when confronted by them.

The patterns by which we as human beings experience life transitions are repeated throughout our lifetime. Whether we are moving from adolescence to adulthood, from the first half of life to the second, or into old age and beyond, the patterns are somewhat parallel. When one studies the many approaches to change and transition we consistently find there are three basic stages to our transitions. While called by a host of names, they can be equally disconcerting whether they are experienced in adolescence or midlife.

FIRST HALF ⇒ MIDLIFE ⇒ SECOND HALF

SEPARATION ⇒ LIMINALITY ⇒ REINTEGRATION

According to the model of psychologist Murray Stein in his work *In Midlife*,[1] the first stage of transition is known as *separation* or *endings*, the second, *liminality*, and the third, *reintegration*. In this chapter we wish to provide a brief overview of the entire midlife process. Each of these individual stages have overlapping yet very distinctive characteristics and tasks which will be detailed in three of the chapters which follow.

SEPARATION

Separation, which is the initial stage of transition is, for those in midlife, the period during which we begin to question our outward roles and the identity we have spent our first forty or fifty years creating. Often we begin to look back at the dream of our early years and come to realize that it may never be fulfilled or, if already achieved, it simply doesn't have the meaning and satisfaction we expected it would. It is an indispensable time which is a harbinger of major change in our life. There are other characteristics found in this stage which will be examined in the next chapter, but separation, like the stages which follow it, has a very specific task which must be accomplished to some degree before the next stage can be embraced.

The Task of Separation

This first stage of midlife is known as separation because a very specific season of our life is ending to make way for a new beginning. To fully embrace that which is to come, we must first say good-bye to and let go of that which "was," that which we are leaving and losing. Thus the task of separation is to discover those losses and to grieve. To fully experience separation, we must stop and recognize that which is passing and admit it will be missed. This might be our role as parent, change of career, or our full head of dark hair.

LIMINALITY

The stage which follows separation is known as *liminality*. This stage is the keystone of midlife and is best described as the moment when we walk through a doorway from one room to another and we are neither in the room we have left nor the room to which we are going. We are in between. Liminality, then, is the stage when we are no longer in the first half of our life; however, we are not yet in the second half. We are no longer what we used to be, but we are not yet what we will become. We are betwixt and between. We are much like the adolescent who is no longer a child but not yet an adult.

The Task of Liminality

For most of us this is one of the most painful stages of any transition and it has for its task the need to simply *embrace* the sense of liminality and to allow ourselves to be in this state of uncertainty, of being betwixt and between. This is the core task of midlife.

REINTEGRATION

Reintegration is the final step between the midlife transition and fully living the second half of our lives. If successfully reached, it is characterized by a newly developed, yet still developing, sense of identity. As we move to our second half of life identity, we will find we are less driven by what people may think of us, and more by a deeper sense of knowing who we are in God's eyes. We recognize that our identity comes not from what we do, but from our simply being a Child of God.

The Task of Reintegration

The task of this final stage of midlife is to develop intimacy with God and Self. From this intimacy we continue to discover this deeper identity within us and thus to move into the second half of life with a revitalized sense of *mission*.

PROCESS REPEATS

Unfortunately, this threefold process is seldom an event which we go through once and for all. We may experience our midlife transitions in different areas of our lives according to the various roles we bear. We may experience a time of transition in our identity as husband, wife, worker, member of a religious community, friend, church leader, or any number of different situations. We will usually go through these same three stages in each transition we experience and the movements may be many. Midlife is a complex journey, with a host of transitions which can offer a multitude of opportunities for pain and growth. Nor do these three stages occur necessarily so clearly or precisely. They interweave and overlap with one another. Yet using these stages as a guide will often help us to identify and clarify the process of midlife as we experience it or are witness to it in those around us.

As we prayerfully move through these stages, we may begin to recognize that in spite of our own uncertainties and turmoil we can have hope that, even though our path is clouded at the moment, we can come into the light with a new meaning for our life.

I will lead the blind on their journey / by paths unknown I will guide them. I will turn darkness into light before them / and make crooked ways straight. [Isaiah 42:16]

4

A View
of the Mountain

We realize that the chapter which follows is the most complex of this book. However, it will provide a useful definition for many of the terms we will use in describing the midlife process and its healing which follow. We encourage readers to grasp as much as they can on its first reading and to return to it when the concepts described are used further on.

To describe something as complex as the universe is an awesome task, if not an impossible one. The best one can do is make an effort to find a small piece which lends itself to description. The task of describing the human psyche is no less awesome. In our previous book, we used Jung's theory of Typology to describe the human personality in terms of four pairs of opposite characteristics: introvert and extrovert, thinking and feeling, and so on. While such an effort can shed much light on human behavior, it still falls far short of a full explanation of our human nature. Any explanation can and will fall short.

We heard it best described by Abbot David Geraets, the head of the Benedictine community in Pecos, New Mexico, with which we are affiliated as oblates. Abbot David compared the effort of describing the human psyche to standing at the foot of a mountain and attempting to describe it. What we describe as we stand there is true and accurate, but it is only one view of the mountain. Were we to walk around the base of the mountain for a while, we would see and thus describe a different perspective of the mountain. Our description would be distinct from the first, yet it would still be accurate. Yet the description would not be a full report of the nature of the mountain, it would be only one view of the mountain.

Thus it is with the description of the human psyche. In creating us in his image and likeness, God has created us an extremely complex and wondrous being. Our description of this awesome creation will, like others, be one view of the mountain. It will be accurate from one viewpoint and helpful when taken from that perspective.

Our human nature and our response to other human beings, ourselves, and God have much to do with our interior life. By interior life, we mean not only the parts of ourselves we know, our conscious, but the parts which are hidden as well, the unconscious. We will explore our conscious and unconscious selves through the psychological concepts of C. G. Jung. By understanding this view of the mountain and how it affects us at midlife, we may come to grips with some of the unseen energies that often seem out of control during midlife.

We believe Paul was deeply in touch with these realities when he wrote what has become known as Paul's prayer in Ephesians 3:

Out of his infinite glory, may he give you the power through his Spirit for your hidden self to grow strong, so that Christ may live in your hearts through faith, and then, planted in love and built on love, you will with all the saints have strength to grasp the breadth and the length, the height and the depth, until, knowing the love of Christ, which is beyond all knowledge, you are filled with the utter fullness of God.

By better understanding our "hidden" or unconscious selves, we may bring to light a new appreciation of why we behave as we do and why we respond in a particular way to certain people. Particularly at midlife we can find in our unconscious a deep source of renewal, growth, strength, and wisdom. Fortunately, this comes at a time when we are called to seek God's Will for us in a totally new way. This call to understand ourselves better at midlife comes as an invitation, and it is a key to growing in intimacy with ourselves and increasing our freedom to love others more intimately.

Our own experience has proven that having an idea of how we are made and the parts of our "psyche" can be of great value when trying to understand our personality in general and our experience of midlife in particular. For this reason, we will begin by offering a model of the human psyche which has helped countless individuals better understand themselves. We will illustrate and define various components of ourselves which we will expand upon in subsequent chapters to give a very useful tool to help us in our self-understanding.

The concepts we will attempt to define in a very simple way are the conscious and the unconscious — both collective and personal — the ego, the persona, the shadow and the Self (or God's Will).

To illustrate this structure, we will use the symbolic shape of the circle divided into two primary parts, the conscious and the unconscious.

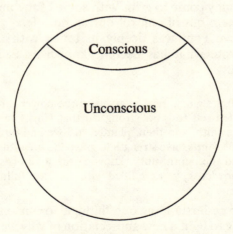

Figure 1: The Psyche

The conscious is that part of ourselves of which we are currently aware. In computer language, it is our current memory bank. At any given moment, when we are awake and alert, we are aware of our body, our physical comfort or discomfort. We are aware that we are a man or woman, a father or mother, husband or wife, and so on. We are attuned to our outward identity. This might be our vocation or our state in life. It is the concept we have of ourselves and the one we want others around us to have.

We are usually mindful of the subject about which we are thinking, the situation in which we find ourselves. This and much more make up our conscious selves.

Yet, as one can see from figure 1, an even larger part of our psyche is our unconscious. Many theories maintain our unconscious makes up 90 percent of our psyche. The unconscious is that vast reservoir of information and energy of which we are not currently aware. It includes all of the material which was at one time conscious, but no longer is. This could include forgotten information or knowledge which was repressed or suppressed because it was too painful or threatening.

The unconscious also contains information, ideas, and stimulus which was never made conscious for a host of reasons. Perhaps "subliminal" information which was too subtle for the conscious mind to notice, yet became a part of our unconscious. After we describe the Ego, we will notice other ways information finds it's way to the unconscious.

As one can see from figure 2, the unconscious is also made up of two separate components. Within us we find the *personal* unconscious and the *collective* unconscious.

THE PERSONAL UNCONSCIOUS

The personal unconscious is that part of our unconscious which is unique to each of us due to our individual life experience. It contains the material which comes from my personal memories, my own background education and experiences. My perception of teachers and other authority figures are developed from my own experience of authority and teachers. My experience of change and rejection are affected a great deal by my own background. No one else has lived life quite like me and thus no one shares the contents of my personal unconscious.

THE COLLECTIVE UNCONSCIOUS

The collective unconscious is the part of our unconscious which we share with all of humanity. It is a part of our unconscious

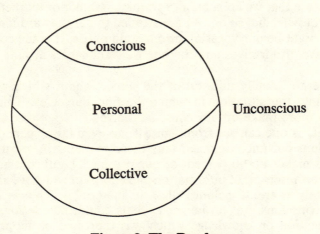

Figure 2: The Psyche:
(with Personal and Collective Unconscious)

which "comes with the package." We are born with a certain set of preconceived ideas and impressions as a result of all of the life which has gone before us. The theory of the collective unconscious is opposed to the idea that human beings are born with a "clean slate." On the contrary, Jung did extensive travels and research to authenticate his theory of the collective unconscious. He investigated cultures in the far reaches of the world and studied their customs, folklore, and religions to identify the common symbols and ideas that were universal to all walks of life. He found that certain ideas and customs were indeed generic no matter where one traveled. Certain symbols meant the same in the furthermost corners of Africa, South America, North America, Europe, and the Far East. The symbol of the circle is almost universally the symbol of wholeness and completeness. The symbol of water is a common symbol of cleansing and new life in nearly all cultures and customs. Certain concepts of mother and father, men and women, children and passages from one age to another are found in all areas of the world and can be traced back through history in myths, and in religious customs, and scripture.

From this fascinating research Jung deduced his concept of

the collective unconscious or objective psyche. He concluded that as part of the human condition we bring along certain primitive baggage in our unconscious upon which our personal experience of life builds. He called these building blocks "archetypes," and found that their energy has a tremendous effect on our behavior and the structure of our unconscious. He further learned that during the second half of life there emanates from within us a need to make conscious the source of this archetypal energy. It is as if a significant cause for much of our behavior has been hidden, and now demands recognition and integration into our conscious lives.

While we will discuss the archetypes and their effects on us in more detail in chapters 7 and 9, it may be helpful to have an idea of how they form the building blocks of our significant ideas and attitudes. The essence of the theory considers the archetypes, which are found in the collective unconscious, to be the core of many concepts we develop during our lifetime. It is as if our personal experiences of life "cluster" around the energy of the archetypes which then form the core of our attitudes. This has been aptly described by the illustration of a magnet placed beneath a sheet of paper with metal shavings on the top. The metal shavings cluster around the poles of the magnet and form a certain pattern around them.

Let us use, for example, the archetype of the mother. This is one of the universal ideas that humankind shares in common. One might say the Mother archetype, with which we are born and which resides in our collective unconscious is the magnetic pole for the experiences of life which are related to the idea of "mother." The total of our collective and personal experiences is known as the "complex." The complex is not used in a pejorative or negative sense here. It simply describes the core archetype surrounded by the cluster of personal experiences to make the whole. Thus the experiences of our own mother and others who represent the mother role in our lives are clustered around this Mother archetype, and the composite or complex will have a tremendous effect on our overall attitude about mothers. Indeed, for a woman the mother complex may well affect the sort of mother she may become; for all of us the complex will affect the way in which we will relate to others whom we consciously or unconsciously perceive as "mother figures."

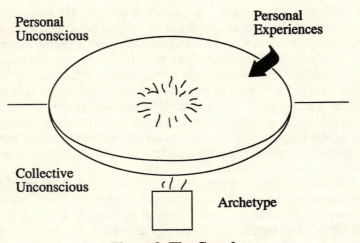

Figure 3: The Complex

The number of complexes we carry is limitless. Each of us has a father complex as well. We also have complexes relating to childhood, authority, anxiety, inferiority, power, God, and others. Again, please recall that the word *complex* is not used in a negative sense. The word *complex* and the complexes themselves are neutral in nature, neither good nor bad. They can, as we will see, become destructive and need to be given attention especially at midlife when many of the complexes we have ignored or repressed in the first half of life begin to demand attention from us. When they remain unconscious, these complexes can be expressed in highly charged ideas and emotions. They act as autonomous personalities within the psyche.

THE EGO

Both the conscious and unconscious have a central force or archetype. We will talk later of the center of the unconscious, but the center of the conscious is the ego.

The Latin word *ego* means "I." As the center of consciousness, when any of us speak of *me* or *I*, it is the ego who both speaks and speaks of itself. To the ego, it is the whole self. The ego or consciousness tends to ignore the balance of the psyche,

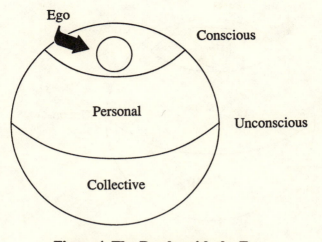

Figure 4: The Psyche with the Ego

which is comprised of the unconscious. To the ego, consciousness is all there is, especially during the first half of life.

Here again, we must avoid negative connotations normally associated with the ego. The ego is not bad. In fact, the ego is the depository of the main gift God has given humanity which separates us from the rest of the animal kingdom: *free will.* The ego is the dwelling place of our will, our ability to choose, freedom itself. Decisions are made by the ego. When we choose our behavior, we do so with the power of the ego. The ego is also the gatekeeper. As the gatekeeper, the ego decides what information will come into consciousness. We are deluged with stimulus and information all the time. Our senses alone would be overwhelmed if we tried to make conscious all of the sights, sounds, and ideas that come our way every waking moment. Thus it is the role of the ego to decide which stimulus is made conscious and which is not, but the majority fall into some complex of the unconscious.

The ego has its own idea of who we are. The ego, as we have said, tends to think of itself as the totality of the psyche; thus when we are thinking of ourselves, we are thinking of what our ego believes ourselves to be. This is one form of our identity, our ego identity. That which our ego thinks us to be. If

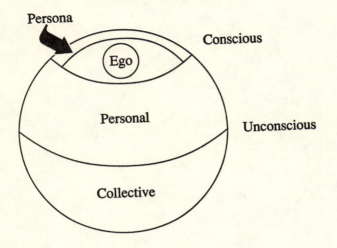

Figure 5: The Psyche with the Persona

we were to sit down and share deeply who we are, we will be sharing our conscious identity formed by our ego. It is vital to healthy functioning in the world to have a strong and positive ego identity — who we think ourselves to be. Yet there is another outward identity as well.

THE PERSONA

As strong and positive as our ego identity may be, we cannot allow all the world to totally see this identity. For this reason, we develop another identity which we present to the world. This is our persona or mask (more usually, a number of masks according to our roles).

The persona is our public self, the self on view for all to see, yet it is not the total or real self according to the ego. The persona is a quite natural and necessary defense of the ego. Were the ego to be totally transparent, we would appear to society to be an extremely unbalanced, unstable, and poorly adjusted individual. Within our conscious identity, we know there resides a frightened little boy or girl who is tempted to cry and go to pieces when things don't go our way. There is also a wild man or woman who craves to rant and rave when we are hurt or threatened. There is also an idiot who seems to want to behave in the silliest and even most bizarre ways at times. Here we discover parts of our ego identity which we cannot let the world see. The components of each individual's conscious identity hidden by the persona will vary dramatically.

Perhaps we have met individuals with weak or damaged personas. We can be with them for a short time and we seem to see their inner self, their brokenness, neediness, and fears. We are often disconcerted when we meet such a person because they are not living up to the behavior society expects of them. Society does not want to see inside of us. Society expects to see the persona.

In closer friendships or relationships we may have less of a mask and show more of our genuine self to another. We *need* relationships like this in our life. It is unhealthy to perceive that we are only as much as we show the world in our persona. As we shall see below, this is what Fritz Kunkel called *egocentricity*.

The persona helps the ego negotiate with the outside world. It is the persona which helps us live out our roles in life, our vocations, our parenting, our state of life. Society expects a doctor to have a certain persona, and thus doctors adapt to that persona. For myself, Bob, as an executive, I was expected to be ruthless in my competition with my peers and follow certain supervisory skills. This was the persona of my career and one to which my ego readily conformed.

Mothers and fathers likewise tend to conform to a certain role which is expected of them. Living in a civilized society demands certain personas from its participants and as such, a persona is a healthy adaptation.

A healthy persona involves being aware of my strengths and weaknesses. My expectation of myself needs to be grounded in the reality of my personality or my persona will become unbalanced. If I am so caught up in my roles in life, I may begin to identify totally with those roles. Even though they are important, in reality, there is much more to our personality.

If lawyers or police officers bring their professional persona home with them, they may be in for a lot of trouble (or their family may be in for trouble). We need to learn to put our work roles aside and allow ourselves to get in touch with and respond to our deeper, truer nature — especially at midlife.

EGOCENTRICITY

The risk in the relationship between the ego and the persona is that the ego may begin to really *believe* the persona. When the ego identifies too strongly with the mask it has created, it tends to deny those less desirable characteristics of consciousness and we fall into the trap of egocentricity. As such, the persona becomes harmful as the ego sees it as true and the sense of healthy balance is lost. The person who becomes obsessed with his or her outer identity will deny his or her own conscious fears, uncertainties, and weaknesses — it is this person who will insist that "what you see is what you get." There is nothing inside, nothing more to reveal, nothing they fear, nothing they seek other than what they commonly show the world. Fritz Kunkel wrote extensively on this subject and further defined certain categories of egocentricity and the characteristics associated with each. We will offer only a brief definition of them. They are the Clinging Vine, the Turtle, the Star, and the Nero. Normally, none of us fully embrace a single one of these patterns, but often we can see aspects of ourselves within them.

The Clinging Vine describes the persons who rely on others for help rather than stand on their own. They may act helpless or appear to be suffering in order to appeal to the sentiments in another. They are overly dependent upon the help of others and may have a difficult time developing their own power to live independently.

The Turtle retreats from life. Such persons may hide away in their shell to avoid the pains and disappointments of life. They may suffer feelings of inferiority and doubt their own ability to fulfill certain necessary tasks.

The Nero wishes to dominate people and situations. They may go about things harshly and not be easily discouraged or disappointed by defeat or opposition. This person is usually oriented to his or her own need for personal power.

The Star believes they are a "very important person." This type demands much attention and recognition by others. They believe they should have the limelight at all times and they feel deserving of the praise and service of others.

We recommend the selected writings of Fritz Kunkel[1] for those interested in further reading on this interesting concept.

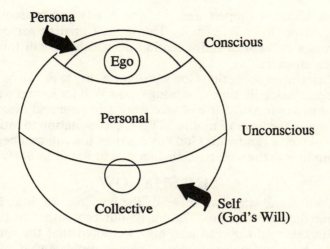

Figure 6: The Psyche with the Self or God's Will

THE SELF

As we said earlier, both the conscious and the unconscious have a central force or energy or archetype. The center of the conscious is the ego. Likewise, the center of the unconscious is the Self — or, as we would prefer, God's Will. The ego would have us believe that it is the center of the psyche, while, in fact, the Self is the center of our entire personality.

It is of the Self which Paul seems to speak when he says, "It is no longer I who live, but Christ who lives within me." Here we find not the transcendent God in heaven, but rather the Will of God for ourselves; our own rich unique identity that comes from being a Child of God. It is the Self, the Archetype of God, that we find at the deepest core of our being. It is here we find the deepest desire of our heart and the divine spark that calls us to unity with God. Here we find the call of God to draw us to himself.

While there is certainly evil to be found in our unconscious, we do not find evil at the core of the human being, rather we find goodness and the divine will for us. (We will discuss the concept of original sin in more detail in chapter 7.) In understanding the Self, we find the wonderful challenge of midlife: to get in touch with this deepest desire of our hearts and consequently to discover God's Will for us. This is the Christian perspective of Jung's concept of individuation on which we will touch in future chapters.

Certainly discovering God's Will is no easy task. We have often spent half a lifetime obscuring God's Will for us and we may not uncover it easily. It will take work and pain and discovery. But this is the work of midlife. This is the invitation to intimacy with ourselves and with God. To discover his will and begin to act upon it is the vocation, challenge, and joy of midlife.

THE SHADOW

You will recall when we spoke of the persona, we described it as our outward identity. The image our ego wishes to project out to the world. Recall also how we noted that the ego acts as the censor of consciousness. The ego decides what will become conscious and what will not. One of the primary criteria the ego uses to make this decision is whether an idea, temptation, or attitude is compatible with the persona. For example, let us assume one has developed the persona of a very honest, righteous person. When thoughts, ideas, or temptations are presented to the ego which are incompatible with this persona, say a temptation to lie or steal, the ego will deny them, thus screening them from consciousness and relegating them to the personal unconscious where they become part of a complex or cluster of similar material constellated around a core archetype (such as the Thief archetype). This unconscious material becomes part of an even larger complex or cluster known as the shadow.

The shadow is comprised of all of the energy, ideas, behavior, temptations, thoughts, experiences, attitudes, feelings, events, qualities, weaknesses, memories, fantasies, drives, among other things, which the ego has decided are not compatible with the identity it has created (i.e., the persona) and thus believes are not part of ourselves. One could say that structurally the shadow is a complex of complexes because it contains all of the complexes our ego finds incompatible.

While these qualities and material are certainly a part of our hidden self or our unconscious, as we will see later, we rarely see them in ourselves, but we certainly see them in other people.

In fact, the shadow has been called the archetype of the Other Person.

PROJECTION

As we will explore in much more detail in chapter 7, the fascinating concept of projection is a tool of the psyche seemingly designed to help us recognize the unappreciated qualities of our shadow. When we hurl a projection, we are seeing a hidden part of ourselves in the mirror of someone else, and seeing that quality has a strong emotional effect upon us. For example, those individuals mentioned above who have developed the honest, self-righteous persona may find themselves strongly repulsed when they come across one they suspect of being dishonest. They may be enraged or furious when one of their children seems to cheat or tell a lie. At its essence, they are seeing their own repressed dishonesty and are projecting it on the "other person." This is certainly not to say lying or cheating is good, rather our own response, if out of proportion to the circumstances, may be a sign pointing to some of the same qualities in our own life. The dishonesty in us may take a much different form from that of the person being projected upon, but it is there nonetheless. We deny it in ourselves, but see it clearly in others.

Likewise, projections can be positive. That is, if we have developed a negative persona, for example, one with a low self-image, the hidden parts of the unconscious may be very positive characteristics repressed by the ego as incompatible with its negative identity. Thus they may see in others the positive qualities they have hidden in themselves and find themselves very attracted to these others. In fact, as we will see, all infatuations and romantic love are the result of positive projections.

Projections are a natural part of living and we are projecting all of the time. The question has been raised that it is not a matter of "if" we are projecting, but "what" we are projecting. Furthermore, projections are a tool of the unconscious and thus can be very helpful in enabling us to see the "hidden self" that Paul exhorts to grow strong. It is our prayer as well that as we delve into these concepts more deeply, your hidden self will grow strong.

The structure of the psyche is an extensive topic of study and integration. We have set forth some very basic concepts and have simplified them to give you, the reader, a brief, but by no means complete, understanding, and to help in your understanding as we use them in chapters which follow. We encourage further reading and study of this fascinating topic to fully understand the midlife process of transformation. These concepts, when applied to our life in a concrete way can be valuable tools to more deeply understand the meaning of self intimacy, intimacy with others, and, most importantly, intimacy with God.

5

Separation
and Endings

When we spoke of *persona* in chapter 4, we described it as the identity we establish for the outside world to see. Each of us has and always will have a persona to protect our ego from displaying the parts of our conscious and unconscious selves that we cannot allow others to see. The development of a persona is a healthy, normal part of the human condition, and we spend the first half of our lives building this sort of "mask" to help us get through life. The difficulty lies in the fact that during this first half of our lives, the development of the persona is greatly affected by what others think and our need to please them. This is particularly true of our parents, and most notably true of our parent of the opposite sex.

Before we discuss the subject of separations and endings, let us invite you to do a short reflection which has proven to be helpful for many.

Think of the parent of your opposite sex. That is, men think of your mother and women your father. Next, describe the characteristics, career, and lifestyle you think would be that parent's *ideal* for someone of your sex. In other words, a man should describe what he thinks his mother would see as an ideal man, and a woman should describe what she thinks her father would describe as an ideal woman. It doesn't matter if it is accurate or not or if others (including that parent and/or your brothers and sisters) would agree with your assessment. What is important is your perception of that ideal. The description of that parent's ideal should include the work, education, lifestyle, family, values, and so on of someone of your sex. Do that now before you go on. It might be very helpful to write out your answers.

PERSONA DEVELOPMENT

If you did this exercise, reflect now on how your own life during the first half was similar to the ideal you believe to be that of your parent described above. For me, Bob, my mother encouraged a very strong work ethic. When I was eleven, I came home from school and discovered my mom had found a paper route for me. Actually, she didn't *find* it, she decided our rural neighborhood didn't have a paper route and called the newspaper to see if her son could start one. (My own kids could tell you the story of how many bitter cold and snowy days I walked along those country roads serving papers — but that's a story for another day!) When May came each year, Mom would let me know which farms in the area were hiring for the summer. I learned quickly that a great deal of a man's measure is found in what he does. That work ethic instilled by my mother's words and reinforced by my father's life was a driving force in my own life for my first forty years and affects me yet today.

I, Carol Ann, had a working mother. My father made it clear he much preferred she stay at home in the roles of wife and mother. While this was a rather negative message for me, I spent the first twenty years of my own marriage at home, in the wife and mother roles.

I recall consciously wanting to spend as much quality time as possible with our children. I held several volunteer roles while they were growing up, but my day usually revolved around being home for the children when they left and returned in the afternoon. I don't regret my choices for that time of my life, but I can see today how much my father's attitude influenced my decisions. Similarly, I am happy with the change of roles in my life today. Writing and presenting retreats and workshops on topics such as this one have been experiences of growth and development. I am recognizing and applying some long suppressed gifts within myself.

None of this is to say we are not deeply affected by our parent of the same sex as well, but in the long run, we tend to live our lives much as we *unconsciously* believe would meet the approval of the opposite-sex parent. Should we not have an opposite-sex parent in our formative years, we would likely select a surrogate, perhaps an older brother or sister, aunt or uncle or neighbor.

Unattainable Ideal

Should we be unable to live out that parent's ideal, we might often find ourselves distressed that we could not do so. For example, the woman whose father's ideal was wife and mother may find herself greatly distressed that she must work outside the home and cannot fully live out that ideal by being home each day for the children. Likewise, the woman whose father affirmed a rewarding career outside of the home may feel trapped during years that she must be at home with her children.

Individuals who pick up messages which impose unrealistic or unattainable goals might also experience unexplainable stress as they continue in roles which they unconsciously believe would not meet that parent's expectations.

At Midlife

During the early stages of midlife we usually begin to question our identity. There is the sense that there is much more to us than what we have previously discovered and now show the world. We get an inkling that there is something more, a deeper identity to be found within us. This is an opportunity to explore the expectations we have developed of ourselves to be sure they are grounded in reality, so that we are not totally caught up in our roles in life. Those roles could be businessman, church leader, wife, father, provider, and so on. They surely are an aspect of who we are, but not the whole picture. We are much more, and at midlife we delve into our truer self as we begin the process of individuation. Fr. John Welch in his book *Spiritual Pilgrims* reflects on this process.

The result of the first phase of the individuation process (first half of life), must be a strong ego-consciousness with a well developed persona. Without this the result, the second phase of the individuation process cannot begin. Someone who has not successfully accomplished the outer journey is not ready for the inner journey. Often people will arrive at the second half of their lives without a comfortable persona or a healthy ego. In this situation contact with the unconscious has to wait until consciousness can be shored up.[1]

BREAKDOWN OF THE PERSONA

This experience of questioning our identity is the beginning of a process of differentiation where we sense and finally know that we are separate and distinct from the roles we play and the personas we wear. This process is part of the first stage of midlife, or separation, and is known as a "breakdown of the persona." Its presence signals the second phase of the individuation process (our second half of life). We begin to see more and more the discrepancy between the person I have shown the world and who I really am inside. To work through this frequently painful encounter in our lives, the help, wisdom, and listening of a friend, spouse, or spiritual director can be very beneficial. In the depth and trust of these kinds of relationships we are able to put masks aside and be loved and accepted for ourselves at the same time.

This is the beginning of the wonderful grace of midlife. This is the initial invitation of intimacy with ourselves, the invitation to discover. To discover a deeper, truer self which lies at the core of our being. Here, we discover not only our true and authentic identity, but, through time, within that identity we can find God's Will for us. At this stage, the search for the Holy Grail begins.

ENDINGS

In this initial stage of midlife transition we also begin to look at the events, roles, and relationships that are changing or coming to an end. Our children are often leaving the nest or at least needing us much less than in their earlier years. We may have lost one or both of our parents, or we may be ending a marriage in divorce or separation. We may often feel gripped with a deep sense of loss. While sometimes our losses are conspicuous, at other times the nature of our losses is less clear.

DREAMS VERSUS REALITY

During this step of separation we may look at the disparity between reality and the dream or dreams we had for our life when we were young adults; the dream of our first half of life. We may have dreamed of being a Wall Street tycoon or being a successful writer or owning our own business or working with the poor around the world. During the process of assessment, it is important to recognize that sometimes our dreams and choices of marriage, family, or career reflect the expectations of our culture or our parents more than our own personal desires. At times these dreams are very unconscious decisions that may need to be revisited.

As we now reflect on the first half of our life, we may ask ourselves, "Do I need to modify my dream?" or "Is it a realistic dream for me at this stage of my life?" There may be a deeper ambition or call that comes to the fore which we have ignored. We are not called necessarily to disregard or abandon the dream of our first half of life, but to reevaluate it and, if necessary, to change it or be more realistic about it.

The Woman's Dream

This may be especially true for women. Sometimes a woman may put her own dream aside to support her husband's dream. Her own dream may have become lost in this process. At midlife she may come face to face with this reality, especially as her role of mother changes and the children no longer require her full energy and attention. Or it may be that she has chosen a career based on others' expectations and not according to her own dream.

Have you ever sat down and really questioned what you want to do with your life? Reevaluating your dream whether a man or a woman doesn't mean that your past should be eschewed or degraded. We must trust that our dreams and the way we lived them out were appropriate for that time in our lives. Yet there may well be a new dream to pursue for the second half of our lives. Self-examination in light of our doubts can cause us to question our previous choices and commitments, and the process can be exhilarating as well as frightening. Through this very necessary questioning-and-reflection stage of midlife we grow in self-intimacy and become better able to make the appropriate choices for the second half of our lives.

Revisiting Dreams for Married Couples

Revisiting dreams for individuals can be a very difficult process and sometimes unsettling, but for husbands and wives it can prove a very valuable thrust at midlife. Does our dream need to be revisited and revised to be more realistic and meaningful for this stage of our lives? For couples, as for all, this needs to be a time when prayer and discernment become a deep part of determining their choices for the future. In our marriage relationship we need to foster openness, honesty, and trust. Neither spouse can change in a marriage without affecting the other partner. Communication is essential during this and all stages of midlife, especially if intimacy is to grow in the relationship. Are we willing to openly and honestly divulge our dreams to one another? Typically, during the beginning of the midlife transition, we may not know our dream for the second half of our lives. This is an area worthy of the couple's deep discussion and contemplation as they move forward on their journey. Yet it can be a difficult area to search and discuss. What if our dreams are not compatible? How do we give one another the support and encouragement they need if we find a conflict as to how to live out those dreams together?

There are no easy, clear-cut answers to these questions. There is a vital need to be open and honest in our dialogue as well as a need to be flexible as the new dreams solidify. We will each need to view the choices and options open to us not only individually, but how they affect our relationship as a couple.

QUESTIONING

The separation stage of midlife can be a time of questioning. Questioning our career, our relationships, our marriage, the very meaning of life. We also cross-examine our belief systems, including our concept of right and wrong, our political and even religious beliefs. Our relationships and careers can be going very well, yet we can still experience a deep questioning in these areas. Questioning and reflecting can lead to the change and reorientation that is needed for the successful fruition of the second half of life. As we saw in chapter 1, we cannot live our second half of life the same way we lived our first half. If we attempt to do so, we will find that we become stagnant, depressed, and the victim of much inner turmoil. Our psychological and spiritual growth will become stale and boring. As we will see clearly later, this is not to say major changes in career or lifestyle are inevitable. Yet the reevaluation of our motivations and choices is a necessary element in the midlife transition.

DISILLUSIONMENT

The separation stage of midlife can be a time of phenomenal disillusionment. Disillusionment with ourselves and others and with the "system." We may face our own brokenness and failures and see more vividly our inner poverty. It is very stressful dealing with others' expectations as well as our own, We may begin to realize we can't meet the high expectations placed upon us, and then become disappointed with others and disenchanted with ourselves.

FACING MORTALITY

During this stage of separation we face our mortality. In our society youth is idolized. The young often do very daring things we wouldn't think of doing at middle age. When we are young, there is an underlying sense that we are going to live forever. Death is rarely in the foreground of our thought. This is part of the sunrise mentality of which we spoke earlier. Television, movies, and advertising portray an ideal of being young, having sex appeal, and of material consumption.

Maturity and aging are something many people fear and are unable to face in a wholesome manner. When we look in the mirror and see the wrinkles and gray hairs or a growing bald spot, we can choose to acknowledge our age, or unconsciously deny it.

I, Bob, recall a time on vacation a few years back and rushing to a store to check on a purchase before going home. Carol Ann was waiting for me by our suitcases. As I rushed past a shop, a young man who was "huckstering" to get people inside spoke to me: "Take a minute to come in and look Pops." I thought to myself, Pops! He called me Pops! By the time I got back to Carol Ann, she could see that I was visibly upset. "What happened to you?" she asked. "I'm only forty-three years old and some kid called me 'Pops'!" I told her. She had a hearty laugh at my expense and, whenever I get too serious now, she too will call me Pops. For the first time, that youngster put me in touch with my own aging and mortality.

We can deny our mortality or rationalize it away temporarily. At midlife we are called to face our ultimate death. We will not live forever. However, as Christians, our faith in an afterlife should give us a distinct advantage in coping with our mortality here on earth. Coming to grips with this perspective can help us to appreciate the present moment and life more fully today.

So do not worry about tomorrow: tomorrow will take care of itself." [Matthew 6:34]

ADULT CHILDREN

A typically disturbing dimension of this separation at midlife is dealing with our adult children. As our role of mother or father changes and our young adult and adult children no longer depend upon us as they did in the past, we may find releasing them a joy as well as a difficulty. We are still parents but our roles have changed drastically as our children grow older, more independent and leave the nest or go off to college. Many couples experience tension and disagreement in their relationships with their young adult children. As parents, we don't always agree upon how the particular situations should be handled. There may be a difference of opinion or values. One parent may want to be more flexible while the other more strict. Many times we find ourselves on opposite sides of the fence in dealing with our adult children. This can often be the greatest area of conflict between parents, but these differences need to be discussed and resolved.

As parents we may examine the way we relate to our adult children. Are we giving them enough room to develop self-discipline and autonomy? Growing into responsible adulthood involves exercising one's right to learn by making one's own mistakes. We need to learn to relate to them increasingly as adult to adult rather than parent to child. Granted, we will always be their parents, but as each of us grows, our relationships must also grow.

Most adult children have to leave home emotionally as well as physically before they develop the ability to relate to parents as adults. We may need to let go of false assumptions that make us take the blame for all of our children's problems. When the inevitable crisis arises, don't panic. Whatever we do, we must avoid rupturing the relationship by heavy-handed or manipulative methods. We must talk with our spouse about the feelings we may be experiencing that accompany this major shift in our role as parent. None of us want to see our children make mistakes or have major disappointments and hurts in their life, yet mistakes are an inevitable part of their own growth, just as they were for ourselves. Releasing our adult children into God's care and praying for them daily can help our own growth process as well as theirs.

OUR OWN PARENTS

Midlife is a time when the health of our own parents may begin to fail. To watch our once vital parents slowly lose their independence and freedom can be a painful experience. As they deteriorate beyond their ability to care for themselves, many options come our way. We can invite them to move in with our own family, or watch as they go off to live with our siblings or other relatives. We might also find a nursing home or an alternate care home for them. Our own financial situation as well as the psychological effect such a decision may have on our parents and the rest of the family are all considerations we confront at this time.

Such difficult choices often come at a time when many transitions are taking place in our lives. We may have only recently found new financial as well as personal freedom by having tuition bills end and children leaving the nest. We may have long anticipated this freedom as a way to change our lifestyle. Perhaps we planned to go back to school or travel or buy a smaller (or larger) home. We may suddenly find ourselves being asked to put all of that aside for the benefit of our parents or our spouses' parents. Putting these plans and freedoms aside is not to be taken lightly as doing so may well affect how we relate to the care-giving of our parents.

There are no clear-cut choices which will be right for every family. We need to be able to talk about the frustration, guilt, and sorrow that may be a very real part of our inner stirrings at this point in our life. Many of our emotions will be tied to the relationship we have had with our parents over the years and our ability to cope with their disabilities. We need to think out all of the options, and the use of a third party, especially a professional counselor can be extremely valuable during the decision making process. These decisions must not be made hastily while under duress. If, due to a sudden illness of a parent, a quick remedy must be found, it should be clear to all that the solution is only interim, until all parties can come to a more permanent decision.

THE TASK OF SEPARATION

What is the task of this stage of midlife and how do we work through it? The task is to *discover* and *to grieve over our losses.* This is easier said than done. This is a process which requires time to successfully work through. To rush through it can be as dangerous as not pursuing it at all. The areas in which we feel grief stricken are the very crosses that will bring us new life. New life in our own identity, with others and in our relationship with God.

At midlife a part of us is dying and changing. We are no longer who we used to be. A part of us feels dead and, in fact, a part of us is dead. Each person needs to prayerfully ask the question, "What is the area in my life over which I need to grieve?" In the words of Murray Stein:

the person needs to identify the source of pain and then to put the past to rest by grieving, mourning, and burying it. But the nature of the loss needs to be understood and worked through before a person can go on.[2]

But this can be a slow and painful process. It is often difficult to come face to face with the losses in our lives. We tend to deny that anything is really passing. If we are honest, we can touch the loss we will experience as our children leave our nest; our loss as we move from friends or they move from us. The pain we experience as we observe our body slowly decline, as we come to grips with our diminishing beauty or strength. Yet facing these losses is a necessary and essential task as we move forward.

Grief is a normal and natural reaction given to us by God to help heal us. Just as a fever is curative to the body, grieving is curative to the soul. Grief cannot take its natural course when we think that our grief is abnormal, that we are odd, or that no one ever grieved as heavily before. Grief has its own unique rhythm, an ebb and flow that cannot be confined or directed by our willpower. We cannot get over our grief by telling ourselves it will not bother us. Feelings have a lot of energy behind them and we cannot *think* our feelings away. One way of expressing our grief is by talking with a close friend or confidant, someone who will listen and not try to give us a lot of answers. Such a person will allow us to express our grief and loss and won't be uncomfortable with the pain themselves. Talking puts us in touch with our feelings and a good listener can be of tremendous help through this crucial phase of grieving.

This process of grieving can leave us emotionally and physically fatigued. We are tempted to give little attention to ourselves physically. Regular exercise and balanced nutrition can be a very valuable focus during the second half of our lives. Exercise induces relaxation and can rejuvenate us mentally, physically, and even spiritually.

During a difficult time of stress in my life, I, Carol Ann, would swim a few miles each day. It seemed to be the only thing that kept me going and the warmth of the water and the rhythm of my body movement had a very soothing and healing effect. I have continued daily physical exercise ever since and I find it a significant part of my day just as is my time of prayer.

FIVE STAGES OF DYING

In their book *Healing Life's Hurts*,[3] Dennis and Matthew Linn describe Elisabeth Kübler-Ross's five stages of dying[4] and relate them to the stages of forgiveness. We believe these same five stages can be helpful in working through the process of separation at midlife. As with any process, nothing is universal, but these five stages may be of value to you on your journey.

Denial

The first stage is denial. At a time in our life when we are experiencing so much change, we may unconsciously deny there is anything in our life which we are losing. It may be very obvious to others but unclear to ourselves. We may have a suspicion but be unable to consciously deal with it directly, and so may push it even further into the unconscious, and use the defense of rationalization or even intellectualization. It may be that we are psychologically unable to deal with the situation head-on at this moment. It is beneficial for us to ask the Lord to show us the area that we most need to deal with at midlife. With the strength and help of Jesus we may be more able to face the situation at hand.

Anger

The second stage is anger. During the transition of midlife anger frequently rises within us. Research has shown that if anger is swallowed long enough the body "may rebel with ulcers, asthma attacks, hypertension, hyperthyroidism, rheumatoid arthritis, colitis, neurodermatitis, migraine headaches, coronary disease and mental illness."[5] In a very real sense, if we do not deal with the pressures of midlife, they deal with us in a physical or psychological way.

What can anger show us at midlife? We may be angry with ourselves, with our husband or wife, with our family. We may become resentful of the meaninglessness of our tasks, of our way of life. We may say to ourselves, "Is this all there is?" or "What more do I want from life? Why am I so dissatisfied?" Anger can be healthy or unhealthy. It can fuel action for change in one's life or it can consume us. Anger can show us that there is something in our life that needs to change. It can also energize us to change what should be changed so that we can live in a better, more loving environment. Anger can pinpoint a fear we need to face and overcome. It can point us toward areas from which we may need to be detached. Am I angry because I no longer feel useful as a mother? Do I feel anger for wasting my life on what seems to be unworthy endeavors? Am I angry at the company for filling my position with a younger person? Is my anger connected to my identity? Is there an unresolved conflict in my marriage or other area of my life?

In *The Dance of Anger*, Harriet Goldhor Lerner discusses the challenge of anger in our lives and how it is a sign worth listening to.[6] Anger may signal we are not addressing important emotional issues at midlife. Our anger may warn us that we are allowing others to do too much for us at the expense of our own growth. She challenges us to look at our anger and to learn what it might be telling us so we don't blame, or try to change others.

Rather, we are called to look at our own way of relating and see where we need to change.

We can tuck things away just for so long and midlife is a time when unresolved conflict can come to the surface and demand attention. If we are attentive and listen to the anger within us, it may pinpoint an area of loss for us.

Bargaining

The third stage of this grieving process is bargaining. "Lord, if you get me over this mountain or problem in my life, I promise to be a better person, to pray more and be more loving to others." Bargaining is primarily a mixture of anger (blaming another and wanting him to change) and depression (blaming myself and wanting to change myself) and the symptoms vary depending upon which emotion is dominant.

Aspects of projection which we will discuss in more detail later can be seen here. I notice a characteristic in another that is hidden in myself. I see it clearly in another but not in myself, and this characteristic really annoys me. At midlife we often demand change of another without really looking at areas of change and growth in ourselves. Midlife is a journey inward, to the center of our soul where God dwells. The areas of bargaining in our outer life may lead us inwardly to areas where God is calling us to let go.

Depression

The fourth stage is depression. When we notice areas in our life that require letting go, we may experience a kind of depression. It is usually difficult to surrender areas of our lives or roles with which we have become comfortable and familiar. But when these roles are no longer appropriate, separation is essential. Depression can be an indicator that there is an area or an attitude in my life that needs to change. Depression is anger turned inward against oneself. When depression is long term, involving suicidal thoughts, or bringing major changes in patterns of sleep or appetite, then professional help is needed. Depression has many serious implications, but if dealt with can lead to new life and inner transformation.

Acceptance

The fifth stage of grieving is acceptance. As we face our losses and go through the grieving process the result is gratitude and an attitude of thankfulness. We come through the grieving process understanding the good that can come through the pain. We begin to focus more on the growth than upon the hurt. We find a new depth of intimacy with ourselves and with God. If we have allowed God to lead and guide us through this time of grieving into new life, we will feel unbound and free to move on in our life to be directed more by God's Will for us.

Grieving is a painful and demanding process, yet at the same time one which gets us in touch with the deeper reality of our true self and a step in the process of individuation.

QUESTION FOR PERSONAL REFLECTION
AND SMALL-GROUP SHARING

Suggested Scripture: John 12:24, 25

> *In all truth I tell you,*
> *unless a wheat grain falls into the earth and dies,*
> *it remains only a single grain;*
> *but if it dies*
> *it yields a rich harvest.*
> *Anyone who loves his [or her] life loses it;*
> *anyone who hates his [or her] life in this world*
> *will keep it for eternal life.*

PERSONAL PRAYER AND REFLECTION
PRELIMINARY NOTE

Place yourself in the presence of the Lord. Know that God is with you as you reflect upon your life. Ask for grace to help you grow as you understand the patterns God is unfolding in your life.

1. Allow the Lord to bring to mind memories of specific endings in your life and how you dealt with them. Some may involve places, people, jobs, or social groups. Do you see a pattern in the way you handle endings?

2. Reflect back to the first half of your life. Recall the dream or ambition you had for your life in your early twenties. What excited you most about your future? How did you expect to see your life unfolding? What was your hope for the future?

Now, review the dream in light of your life today. Has your earlier dream changed or been modified in some way? Does your earlier dream need revision or change? Do you have new hopes and dreams for the future now? What are they? Write them down.

SMALL-GROUP-SHARING QUESTIONS

1. Do I see a discrepancy between the person I have shown the world and who I really am inside? In what ways, if any, am I questioning my identity?

2. What are my hopes and dreams for my future at this stage of my life? How do I feel about that?

3. Have there been moments recently when I have questioned or been disillusioned with my career, relationships, or even my faith? Explain.

4. Am I able to pinpoint an area in my life in which I feel a deep loss? (For example, loss of job, children leaving nest, personal illness, separation or divorce or my own loss of identity.) Have I begun to grieve over this loss? How does that make me feel?

6

Betwixt
and Between

Life is a never ending-series of transitions. Some are small and easy, others are severe and difficult. Some happen gradually while others are sudden and unexpected. One of the life changes we experience is the transition from the womb into the world. Another is the development from an infant to a child who can distinguish its separate identity from its mother. And so the process continues from adolescence to young adulthood and on and on.

Still other psychological and physiological changes continue to unfold as we move toward the symbolic return to the womb at our death. We move into puberty, young adulthood, middle age, our later years, and finally to death itself. As we have said, these transitions or passages follow a similar pattern and the one upon which we focus here is no different. In fact, midlife may encompass many smaller transitions occurring all at the same time.

At some time in all of our transitions, no matter how trivial or dramatic, we find ourselves in a state of "betweenness." When we perform the simple chore of changing from one task to another in our daily routine, there is at least an instant when we are in between our occupations. It is the time when we are no longer doing the old task, but have not fully invested ourselves in the new. In a manual transmission automobile, we experience the same phenomenon when we shift gears. We depress the clutch and move the gear shift to the new gear. For a short time, the transmission is neither in the former gear nor the gear of destination.

Being in between characteristically involves a period of inactivity, a time when it would seem that the former progress is halted or at least held in abeyance. Often it involves a time of decision. Into what gear will we shift? We might ask ourselves following a meeting, "Exactly what will we do when we get back to the office?" Some transitions take much longer than others. The transition from a meeting down the hall or at church down the block would likely be much quicker than the transition from a meeting across the country.

Transition times often seem unproductive in our hurried world. I, Bob, recall once flying halfway across the country simply to fly back from a meeting with one of our corporate officers trying to shorten his transition time. Yet these times can give us an opportunity to slow down and take stock. They often provide a breather and allow us to physically and mentally prepare ourselves for the tasks yet to come or even to take a brief mental vacation or rest. While each of the above are examples of transitions, they are of a much different nature than the transitions of midlife.

MIDLIFE

As our psyche attempts to shift gears during each of our psychological transitions including the shift from the first half of life to the second, it requires a slowing down, a hesitation, a time of coasting to prepare it for this next phase.

This stage of midlife is known as *liminality*. It comes from the Latin word *limen*, "threshold," and is best described as the moment when we are walking from one room to another and find ourselves neither in the room we have left nor the room to which we are going. To use our automotive analogy, it is the time the transmission is in neutral during a change of gears. During liminality at midlife, we experience a pause in our lives. We hesitate, usually unwillingly, as we prepare for the next phase — life's second half.

As a state of life, liminality can be extremely disconcerting and is often experienced as a disconnectedness. Frequently, all we know is that we are no longer the person we previously thought ourselves to be, but we are certain (fairly certain) that we are not yet fully the person we are meant to be. A friend described her life during this time by saying, "I know clearly that who I am today is changing and I will be different in the future, but that is the only thing I am certain of — that I am evolving into a new woman."

The most prevalent feeling at this time is a sense of being in suspension. In the last chapter we spoke of separation coming as a result of a breakdown of our persona, our outward identity. During the period of liminality, we often feel a conviction that there is much more to our identity than we previously thought. We are no longer that same person we were during the past fifteen or twenty years. We are no longer only mother or father. No longer are we simply business person or clergy or sister.

During this time we can find ourselves ambiguous about our identity. Just who are we? A woman at one of our workshops explained it like this. "When I attend the football game, where my husband is coach, I am seen as the wife of the coach. When I attend my children's soccer games, I am the kids' mom. At work, I am the secretary to the boss. I know these are a part of who I am, but there is much more. At this time of my life, I am searching to find my deeper identity." As she spoke there were tears in her eyes. This was a question of utmost importance that needed to be faced.

We may sense untapped potential in ourselves, hidden or even buried from our own sight and reason. But we know it is there, like a buried treasure waiting to be uncovered. What is this source of new life and why is it so hard to find and expose? It is truly a *pearl of great price*. We must seek and search and knock. It takes time to discover and it also takes courage.

VULNERABILITY

During liminality, as a result of our being betwixt and between, we often experience feelings of extreme vulnerability. We sense this vulnerability if someone should attack either our role or our seeming uncertainty about ourselves. Should someone attempt to move us along toward our forthcoming role too quickly or press us to regain our old roles, we may either attack them or withdraw. We may become quite sensitive and in need of additional physical and emotional space. A feeling of emptiness and hollowness can give the appearance of a severe depression. In fact, times of depression in ourselves are often brought about when we are in a quandary about our identity.

Our emotions will call for attention as we try desperately to bring closure to this awkward period. Now, more than ever, we must listen to the yearnings of our inner self.

If we are a wife and mother, we may view our roles as drastically changing. The children we have spent so much of our time and energy raising may be ready to go off to college or may be venturing out on their own. Even if they remain at home, they are getting older and much less dependent upon us. We are likely not needed in the same capacity as only a few years earlier. We may find ourselves bored, angry, or even bitter over our role as wife.

Even if we have an outside job, it may not seem to be fulfilling. We may come to resent our roles of wife and mother and the required constant care and attention of others, including the nitty-gritty of cooking, cleaning, and picking up after a group of increasingly independent "others." Indeed, we may need and desire some time and space for ourselves. Time to discover our own potential which we feel bubbling up from within and longing to be recognized. We might say to ourselves, "What is wrong with me? What do I want from life?" These feelings may have been placed on the back burner for a long time and at midlife demand recognition. If recognized and dealt with, these feelings can help us to channel this energy to deal with the real issues at hand: to discover our potential and find new meaning in who we are and what we do with the second half of our lives.

Sometimes these strong emotions may help us to realize that we may be overly dependent on our spouse. Do we ask him to take responsibility for our choices and decisions when we could make them just as well on our own? How about areas with which we are uncomfortable such as confrontations? Do we take an area of weakness and let our husband handle those situations for us? This is an area many woman as well as men may need to face at midlife. Such admission may produce strong feelings of vulnerability.

Each of us handles midlife issues differently. Much depends

upon our background and our family. How did our parents handle their emotions? How did they condition us to handle our own? Did we learn to recognize and talk about our feelings or were they suppressed and covered over? The emotions we have denied or buried during the first half of our lives will resurface at midlife and demand our attention. Thus one can see why the vulnerability of midlife is as different and unique as each individual.

We may need to withdraw to give ourselves the space we need to discover some inner values we wish to pursue. Often during this time, we will withdraw from some of our optional activities or substitute less demanding enterprises for those requiring higher outputs of energy. One person may need to take up school or volunteer activities to gain space, while these may be the exact same undertakings another must put aside to accomplish his or her goal.

Many churches and volunteer organizations will lose their members at midlife as they seek much needed time to discover their newly emerging identities. When asked to explain their withdrawal, most are unable to give a rational explanation. They simply know they have a strong desire and need for space. We have seen so many people abused by leaders of organizations, especially church groups, when they sought to bow out of responsibilities in an effort to hear the call of midlife. It would seem that the church, more than any, should be sensitive to individuals' needs to grow and change at this stage. Support and encouragement from the church community can help create a healthy atmosphere for change.

We have also seen as an alternative to radical withdrawal the emergence of midlife support groups within churches and organizations. The church can provide the structure and opportunity to encourage its members to share, in a Christ-centered, nonjudgmental environment, the pain and struggle of midlife.

DECISION MAKING

During midlife we feel an often urgent need to make decisions about our life. Our need to make decisions is found in our natural inclination to move away from pain, and this tendency is particularly exacerbated in the Me Generation mentality which influences each of us. It is during the pain and uncertainty of liminality when a host of possible remedies to stop our pain will present themselves. What should we do? Should we get another job, find another city, buy another car, switch to another hairstyle, another wife or husband?

Considering our options in a new set of life circumstances, that is, life's second half, is an important factor during this time; for this reason, we have devoted chapter 12 to the subject of appropriate and inappropriate midlife decisions.

CONFIDENCE

During liminality, we may experience gains and losses in our self-confidence. We might even find ourselves flying high with an inflated idea about our own worth, abilities, or importance. At one moment, we might think we have accomplished our first-half-of-life objective of conquering the world. We believe we *have* conquered the world! At the next moment, we feel deflated and conquered ourselves.

Midlife can be a time of significant self-doubt. What have I done with my life? Has it really been worth it all? If we are able to recognize this, we can see it as a search for our deeper identity, our truer self-worth. Sometimes this anger and pain can be turned in on ourselves. We think if we were better Christians these things wouldn't be so upsetting to us. We think we should be able to be strong, to get out there and beat this!

All of this anger directed at ourselves can bring about depression and even physical illness. Swallowing the emotions, the anger, the loneliness leads to the same thing. Can we be honest with ourselves? Are we able to keep a journal of the feelings churning inside, and what is really going on? Are we able to really pinpoint the source of our anger, guilt, and loneliness?

We can be in so much pain ourselves that we begin to blame others, if married, especially our spouse, for all the emotions we are experiencing. Yet at midlife we are invited to understand that we ourselves are responsible for whatever loneliness, meaninglessness, or other pain we experience at this time.

As part of the questioning of our confidence, we may begin to question our ability to love and be intimate with others. If our marriage is boring, we could blame ourselves. If we are single, we wonder if we could ever have a mate. If we have no close friends, we wonder what we have done wrong. Many celibates have shared with us their own questioning about their decision to choose the celibate life during their midlife years. This is especially so if they have not developed healthy relationships with members of the opposite sex. (Much of this concerns the emerging contrasexual roles at midlife which are discussed in chapter 9.)

DEATH ANXIETY

At midlife we can begin to feel anxiety about our death. While in the separation stage we begin to face our mortality, during liminality we can begin to feel a real sense of apprehension. We may begin to read the death notices in the paper and pay more attention to the ages of the deceased. We may now notice the deterioration of our body. We begin to notice some new wrinkles and wonder if we should stop smiling as much. We may begin to listen more intently to the ads for cosmetic surgery. We are likely to notice our thinning or graying hair and our inability to keep up with the kids or grandkids. Each time we have a pain in our chest we are sure this will be the "big one."

A good deal of this anxiety has to do with our own movement from the sunrise perspective of the first half of life to the sunset perspective of the second half. We are touching our own mortality with the realization that one day we will indeed die.

At the same time we are touching our own *actual* death we are also, in a sense, experiencing a sort of *symbolic*, psychological death. It is as if we are touching the death of what was, that is, our former self, the persona we had developed. With this recognition, there can come an openness and readiness for the new life and identity which is nearing the end of its gestation period. It is important not to run away from this anxiety. It can be beneficial to pray about this and meditate on the reality of our own deaths. Few of us really move toward an acceptance of our own death until actually faced with it. We can, however, move toward a healthy attitude that will allow us to let go of parts of our lives, such as roles, attitudes, and values that are no longer appropriate. This can make way for the new roles, attitudes, and values that will help us successfully navigate the waters of life's second half.

INTIMACY WITH GOD

Frequently during this time there is a new underlying yearning for God that underpins the entire liminality experience. As we will see further in the next chapter, midlife is a time when we develop a deep desire for intimacy with God.

During the stage of liminality, that desire is reborn with a new vigor. We find ourselves quietly called in many ways to turn to our belief in a transcendent God. The God of our childhood beckons us to himself. At one time, we were amazed to learn how many participants in our personality or midlife workshops had experienced religious conversions during midlife. Prayer groups, renewal movements, and twelve-step programs are filled with individuals who are responding to their midlife call to intimacy with God and the journey inward. With our better understanding of the midlife process these common midlife conversions are no longer a surprise to us. This may also help us understand others' search for intimacy with God at midlife.

This is not to say that religious conversion always occurs during midlife. We are called to a *deeper intimacy* with God throughout all of our lives. Yet no matter how close or far away we seem to God, a call to more intensity in our relationship with God will indeed be issued during our middle years. The most pious and prayerful individual alive will hear at midlife a call to a deeper, more intimate relationship with God. It is our experience that perhaps those who consider themselves closest to God often have the most difficulty hearing this call at midlife. It is almost as if we think God should issue this call to the "others," but couldn't mean *me too*! Yet the call issued to each of us is to a deeper conversion, a transformation that will open us to more abundant grace and freedom. It is here that Jesus gently, yet consistently invites us to intimacy with himself.

During liminality, this call may seem quite obscure. We sense there is a call to intimacy, but often at this stage we are unable to discern from where it comes. We may interpret it as a call to intimacy with our spouse or another person. We may respond in a healthy manner or in a destructive manner. Sexual affairs, drug and alcohol abuse are often unhealthy, destructive responses to the deeply spiritual call to intimacy with God gone unrecognized.

METAMORPHOSIS

The caterpillar makes a chrysalis or cocoon when it is time to begin the process of transformation into a butterfly. The process is very slow. During the metamorphosis the chrysalis appears lifeless and dead. This, we know, is only an illusion. It only appears to be dead. During the transition, the animal is in liminality. It is neither a caterpillar nor a butterfly. It is betwixt and between — experiencing the death-to-new-life process.

At midlife, we too experience this process of death and rebirth. In liminality, we are in the process of renewal. We need the time and space to be in between, to let go of what was and prepare for the new life that lies ahead. This painful process doesn't happen instantaneously. The process of brand-new life for humans takes nine months from conception to birth. During that time we are being formed and nurtured in the womb before we are ready to come through the birth canal into the new world.

This cycle of death to new life is difficult and painful. Change does not come easily to any one of us. Even when that change is for the better, there is always a reorientation involved.

In her book on psychological transformation, *The Pregnant Virgin*,[1] Marion Woodman describes this time of liminality very aptly:

It is the twilight zone between past and future that is the precarious world of transformation within the chrysalis. Part of us is looking back, yearning for the magic we have lost; part is glad to say good-by to our chaotic past; part looks ahead with whatever courage we can muster; part is excited by the changing potential; part sits stone-still not daring to look either way.

She goes on to say, "Individuals who consciously accept the chrysalis . . . have accepted a life/death paradox, a paradox which returns in a different form at each new spiral of growth."

TASK OF LIMINALITY — EMBRACE LIMINALITY

Probably the most difficult aspect of this stage is its task. For the task of liminality is to simply embrace its very nature. To allow it to happen to us. To *be* in liminality. To be betwixt and between. To be able to say to ourselves, "I am no longer what I used to be, but I am not yet what I will become, and it's okay!" This is a most difficult task because it simply doesn't feel good at first, or perhaps ever.

We live in a society that does not like pain and has a habit of fixing what is wrong with it. For this reason, we have a craving to get out of this stage. This is when we are most tempted to make dramatic changes in our lives to stop the pain of liminality. We quit our job, have an affair, move to a new location, find a new church, change our vocation, or immerse ourselves in our work to avoid persevering through the pain. Countless devastating life changes have been made in an attempt to avoid this painful experience. Yet a sustained experience of liminality is a prerequisite in order to move into the final stage of midlife transition and, in fact, into the entire second half of life.

THE CORE EXPERIENCE

While liminality is the most difficult and painful part of midlife, it is the most crucial. It is the core midlife experience which alone allows us to successfully move into the second half of life. A significant part of the growth at midlife lies in our need to painstakingly experience this often unaccustomed sense of "in-betweenness" or liminality.

In the first half of our lives, life seems crystal clear, absolute, categorical, black and white. During liminality we obtain a newly found sense of ambiguity or "gray" in our understanding of life and its components. As we move further into the second half of life, we ascertain that life itself is not nearly as definitive as we speculated in our earlier days. In fact, as we will see in reintegration, the final stage of midlife, we learn that life is full of paradoxes and ambiguities. Nothing will ever be quite as certain for us in the second half as it seemed in the first.

TRAINING GROUND

But, if done well, this stage of liminality can teach us to live with this new understanding of life. For this reason, liminality is a training ground for the second half of life. To successfully navigate the gray, yet beautiful waters of life's sunset, we must take with us an appreciation and acceptance of the enigmatic nature of life. If we succeed, this liminality can cultivate in us the mellowness required to gracefully accept our aging and the harmonious wonder life will become. It is this same weathered beauty we notice in those who have aged well. They seem to approach life less intensely and with what we call "good nature."

Indeed, midlife is a fascinating adventure, but more than anything it is a time of preparation. A necessary time which will prepare us for the successful navigation of the rest of our lives. We know by now that such lessons are rarely realized effortlessly. They frequently include failures, false starts, misunderstanding, and, most commonly, pain. Unquestionably, those who have read this far will know by now that painful revelations about themselves are an inherent component of this journey. Now we move to one of the key lessons of midlife — meeting our shadow.

QUESTION FOR PERSONAL REFLECTION AND SMALL-GROUP SHARING

Suggested Scripture: Isaiah 42:16

> *I shall lead the blind by a road they do not know,*
> *by paths they do not know I shall conduct them.*
> *I shall turn the darkness into light before them.*

PERSONAL PRAYER AND REFLECTION
PRELIMINARY NOTE

Say the Holy Name of Jesus several times, slowly and reverently. Feel Jesus' presence within you. Know that he is leading and guiding you with the light of his presence and Spirit.

1. Read again the beginning of Isaiah 42:16. "I shall lead the blind by a road they do not know, by paths they do not know I shall conduct them. I shall turn the darkness into light before them."

In what area of my life do I feel most "blinded" or in liminality? How does this make me feel inside? Do I feel vulnerable? How?

2. During this time of midlife transition, do I see my relationship with God changing? How? Are there moments I feel like God is nowhere to be found or like God has left me in the dark?

SMALL-GROUP-SHARING QUESTIONS

1. In what area of my life do I feel a sense of vulnerability? Does this affect my emotions and confidence about myself? How does this vulnerability make me feel?

2. As I move through this time of liminality, am I experiencing a sense of hopefulness or despair? Share that hope or despair.

3. Have I noticed any anxiety or fear of death occupying my thoughts? How does this occur and how do I feel when it happens?

4. How is God calling me to a deeper intimacy and trust at this time of my life?

5. How do I feel hearing that the main task of this time of liminality is to simply be in the betweenness?

7

Liminality and the Shadow

In chapter 4, when we described the structure of the psyche, we briefly explained the concept of the *shadow*. We described it as the portion of the unconscious in which resides all of the memories, thoughts, experiences, behavior, desires, inferior personality characteristics, temptations, emotions, and ideas about ourselves which are incompatible with the outward identity or persona developed by the ego. Much of what is found in our shadow was at one time conscious, but for many reasons we have either forgotten, repressed, or suppressed it. Some of the contents of the shadow were never made conscious because the ego, as the "gatekeeper" or censor of the conscious, simply screened them out and they became another element in one of the myriad of complexes which reside as a part of the unconscious. Even some of our actual behavior can be denied by the ego and become part of our shadow.

COMPLEX OF COMPLEXES

You will recall that complexes are the cluster of personal experiences which assemble around each of the archetypes which are part of our collective or objective psyche. The shadow itself could be called a "cluster of clusters" or a collection of complexes, all of which our ego cannot hold in consciousness as it finds them threatening to the persona it has constructed for the world. Consequently, the persona and the shadow are compensatory opposites. In other words, the larger or more dramatic or rigid our persona, the more considerable and dramatic will be its opposite characteristics hidden in our shadow.

It is important to understand that the shadow is not negative by definition. In fact, Jung was quite clear that the shadow is amoral. As we will discuss below, the shadow can and does contain quite "positive" energy and characteristics, and even the qualities we would hold as unfavorable can become helpful and positive when properly integrated within our Christian value framework. Our shadow remains harmful only to the extent that it remains unconscious. The contents themselves, properly integrated, can be quite positive, constructive, and life giving.

For example, those who have developed a very aggressive, controlling, and "in-charge" attitude toward life may find their gentle and compassionate characteristics irreconcilable with their self-image. Thus when such emotions, temptations, thoughts, and behavior are presented to their ego, the ego will quickly repudiate and repress them. The ego cannot embrace these tender and warmhearted tendencies as they are irreconcilable with the more aggressive persona it is trying so hard to present to the outside world. As this outward identity amplifies and grows, so does the compensatory shadow side.

On the other hand, the sweet, gentle, "never-hurt-anyone" person may find a very aggressive, controlling personality within the confines of their shadow as a result of years of denial of these characteristics when presented to the ego.

VARIETY OF PERSONAS

At this point it may be helpful to understand that we carry a number of different personas depending on the role we are playing at any given time. We might have one persona for our work environment and another for home. We may function with one set of characteristics at church and another when we have our "parent" hat on. Thus our shadow can be the opposite of the persona I am wearing *at a certain time*. In business we are put in the position of wearing the persona of "boss" one moment, when we are supervising subordinates, and wearing the persona of "subordinate" the next, when we are in the presence of our own boss. The energy required to frequently shift roles can be draining.

In fact, in some instances, what is shadow for one role may be persona for another. I, Bob, experienced this for many years after our conversion and return to the Church. We were quite active in the Marriage Encounter Movement which, while openly speaking of masks, demanded a certain mask of its devotees. One was beseeched to behave in a somewhat ideal manner, being totally attentive to one's spouse and candidly open about the most private facet of our lives and marriage. (Let this not sound negative as this movement gave our relationship and indeed our lives a totally new beginning.) My own more natural, strong leadership qualities were temporarily put aside, and the very qualities I would disdain for myself at work were inspired at our evening get-togethers. This was a rather emotional time in trying to balance these seeming opposite identities. At its deepest though, the shadow will embody the composite opposite of all of our persona or outward identities.

AT MIDLIFE

One of the key characteristics of the betwixt-and-between or liminality stage of midlife, is that this same shadow which we seemed to have successfully kept under control for our first thirty, forty or fifty years, begins to emanate from our unconscious with a new-found energy of its own. It seems we are able to keep the substance of the shadow under control for only so long. The "wonder years" of midlife seem to be the hour preordained by God for us to confront these characteristics as they develop a blooming gusto and potency. It is as if they now refuse to stay in the background and begin to demand attention from us.

Let us take again, for example, the sweet, gentle man or woman who would never hurt anyone. During much of their life, whenever they experienced temptations or actually behaved in an aggressive, hostile, assertive way, perhaps in a fit of anger, their ego would seek to repudiate this experience or temptation. If the ego is successful, the temptation may seem to pass or the behavior may be denied as though it never happened. The energy of the act or temptation does not, as we would like to think, simply dissipate. The psyche hoards this power in its ever-growing inventory of analogous energy in the unconscious, where they are clustered around all of the other related experiences and temptations known as the shadow. This magnetic power center is the archetype. Recall our illustration of the magnet in chapter 4. The magnet, forming the pattern of the metal shavings represents the archetypes or psychic energy with which we are born and the metal shavings, our life experiences. The resultant total is known as the complex and as mentioned earlier, the shadow is a cluster of all the complexes we have denied, rejected, or repressed. While we may be vaguely aware of their existence within us, for the most part we totally deny their presence in both our behavior and our unconscious.

In actuality, if we cannot see our shadow, those around us certainly can. One of the clues we get about the contents of our shadow is when those who know us well describe some of our inconsistent behavior and we cannot believe them. "No," we say, "I never do that! Tell me once when I actually did that! I would never say anything like that!" Unconsciously, we hope the contents of our shadow will remain in quiet isolation forever and that no one will notice. In reality they remain buried within us in a state of *fermentation* or *percolation* until the midlife years when they demand *attention and acknowledgment!* This is when the fun begins!

TOOLS OF THE SHADOW

Our psyche has a wonderful assortment of tools with which it gently or more dramatically encourages us to give attention and acknowledgment to our unconscious shadow. There seems to be a progressive nature to the psyche's use of these tools, each one intensifying in its impact on our behavior and its fervent ability to earn our attention.

Prayer

One way in which we often recognize our shadow is through prayer. Through the daily examination of our actions or quietly meditating we can become aware of hidden parts of ourselves. Recognizing our shadow in prayer requires both an astuteness and sensitivity. Putting time aside each day in a regular ongoing fashion and allowing time for quiet reflection without a lot of words or petitions may help us enter into this realm.

Reading scripture can often put us in touch with qualities we have long denied. We might reflect on Jesus' parable concerning the rich man building new barns to hoard his harvest (Luke 12:16ff). After time, we may tap into our own repressed selfishness and realize that secretly we have hoarded much and fear the poverty to which we are called. We might spend time reflecting on Jesus' frequent admonition of the legalistic Pharisees and encountering our own hidden legalism and judgments of others.

Dreams

A second tool our unconscious uses to introduce us to our shadow is through our dreams. Dreams are the language of the unconscious, and God seems to make effective use of them as compensation for denials of our outer life and to teach us about ourselves. Indeed, scripture tells us how God uses dreams. He spoke to Joseph about taking Mary into his home (Matthew 1:20). In the Old Testament God spoke to many through their dreams: Joseph, Jacob, Daniel, and many others.

Dreams speak in symbolic language and are often difficult to comprehend and decipher. When we are dreaming, we are most often dreaming about hidden parts of ourselves, our unconscious, including our shadow. In other words, each symbol (person, place, or thing) found in our dream is an aspect of our selves. If we learn the language of the hidden psyche, we can learn much of what is "brewing" and seeking our attention from below.

It is interesting to note that the images in our dreams which represent shadow figures are usually of the same sex. A man dreaming about other men is seeing a symbol of his shadow. Likewise, a women dreaming of women is seeing her shadow side. It is most helpful to bring dream symbols into our prayer time and ask the Lord to help us learn what the symbol means. While solid, healthy dreamwork is an entire study in itself, it is helpful to keep a journal of our dreams and to be willing to dialogue with the figures we encounter. We will be surprised to find that the energy from our dream symbols can and will tell us what they have to teach us and how we have failed to acknowledge these parts of our personality.

For those interested in further reading on this fascinating

subject, we recommend *Dreams and Spiritual Growth* by Savary, Berne, and Williams,[1] and *Inner Work* by Robert Johnson.[2]

Projections

A third method is the fascinating concept of *projection*. Projection is the instrument of the unconscious by which we are invited to see consciously the hidden or unacknowledged characteristics of ourselves through the mirror of *other people*. Not only do we see these characteristics in others, but when they are "negative," they have a tremendous ability to irritate and even enrage us. The tool of projection is not unique to midlife, but it is exacerbated by the midlife transition. In fact, whether we are in midlife or not, the characteristics in other people that we most dislike are usually present in ourselves in some similar or related way and we are currently denying them expression or recognition. At midlife these projections can intensify, and we can find ourselves increasingly irritated by others who previously only mildly bruised us.

One of the classic examples of projection at work comes from an individual at one of our midlife workshops whose story we tell with his permission. We will call him Anthony. Anthony told of being at a restaurant one evening with his wife. Across the room at the bar was a man with two young women. He described the man as "womanizing" the young women and it infuriated him. Anthony couldn't take his attention off the man and, while usually quite reserved in his behavior, was tempted to somehow approach the man and "knock his block off." The evening passed. When Anthony was describing the scene at our workshop in context of projection, he asked, "Are you trying to say that what that guy was doing was part of me, and that's why he made me so angry?" Our standard, noncommittal (and safe) response to such questions is "That's the theory." Another workshop participant asked Anthony, "When you see an attractive woman, aren't you sometimes intrigued and perhaps a bit tantalized?" Anthony responded, "Never! I may find a woman attractively dressed, but I would never be attracted in any sexual way!"

Anthony's case was not uncommon. Don't we all have a bit of Don Juan or Jezebel within us? Isn't that attraction to the opposite sex what enables the human race to continue to propagate itself? Anthony's ego so strongly built its persona identity around the idea of a wholesome, righteous man that, when he confronted his shadow side in the form of a Don Juan across the room, he wanted to "knock his block off."

Here was the unconscious using the tool of projection to get Anthony's attention. Without a doubt, in Anthony's effort to live the wholesome, righteous life that he wanted to live, each time such a temptation crossed his mind or tempted him in some other way, he would banish such an impulse to the basement of his shadow.

One might ask, "Well, isn't that the Christian way to deal with such temptations? What is he expected to do, go out and try to seduce every attractive woman he sees?" Certainly not. But is it possible that such a cavalier attitude might affect Anthony's relationship with his wife and with other women, including family members and friends? Might this persona present barriers to the healthy intimacy necessary in each of our lives and especially the intimacy that comes with the midlife invitation? Only Anthony can answer these questions for himself but a healthy reflection on his associated attitudes could prove helpful. We will return to Anthony further on.

While understanding the concept of shadow and projections can help, knowledge alone does little to help us recognize the hidden shadow qualities within us. We are rarely willing to recognize our enemy's traits within ourselves. However, the qualities are often disguised and difficult to see. They seldom appear in others as they appear in us. For example, I may be extremely irritated by others who seem selfish to me, while seeing myself as very unselfish, giving of my time and money to the poor and those less fortunate. However, I may find it hard to see my own selfishness when it comes to holding onto my children and not allowing them to grow as they must. Perhaps my selfishness is in discouraging my spouse from going back to school which would take some of his or her spare time away from me. Yet when I encounter others who appear selfish, I may be excessively indignant and incensed by their behavior.

POSITIVE SHADOWS

We project our "positive shadow" on others as well. If we have constructed a persona which has negative characteristics, we may be strongly attracted to someone who seems to exhibit the positive side of these characteristics. For example, if overly aggressive, pugnacious persons come in contact with our gentle, sweet never-hurt-anyone person, they may deeply admire the person as they see hidden parts of themselves in the mirror of the other.

One form of "positive projection" is believed to be the source of romantic love. (See Robert Johnson's book on the subject.)[3] We spend years looking for someone who seems to make us feel complete by filling in for our own weakness and promptly fall in love with him or her. (Some would say we spend the rest of our lives trying to then change the person into a copy of ourselves.)

RECOGNIZING PROJECTIONS

One of the common questions about projections has to do with those upon whom we project our shadow. We are asked, "Does that make them innocent?" Others will say, "Some people make me mad just because of the way they behave."

First, let us explain that it is said that we *hang* our projections on other persons. They are called "hooks." Now we fully admit that some people are much better hooks than others, but how do we tell the difference between someone upon whom we are projecting and one who is a pain in the neck? Often we can't tell the difference, because we have the habit of projecting our shadow on those who are a pain in the neck to us. But there is a rule of thumb that can be used. We are said to be projecting on someone if our emotional response to them or a situation is *out of proportion* to the circumstances. If someone is doing something which would seem to be reason for us to be mildly irritated, and we are instead, enraged, we are likely projecting. Likewise, a positive projection might be recognized by our excessive reaction — of infatuation or enchantment — to someone's positive quality, admirable though it may be. In either case, we are seeing our own hidden qualities in the mirror of the other.

An example of a negative projection at work was seen by us in a supermarket. While shopping, we noticed a three or four year old snatch a couple of pieces of candy from a large display meant for customers to bag their selection from round bins, which were fortuitously at the eye level of the youngster. When the child went around the corner to his mother's cart, she discovered the evidence in his hand. Rather than putting the candy back and scolding the child or giving him a little *memory* to go with the scolding, the mother seemed to go haywire. She grabbed the child's arm and began moving in rapid circles as she viciously pursued the child's bottom, spanking him unmercifully. She stopped only when she noticed she was drawing an increasingly hostile crowd. It would be rather easy to see that her emotional response was out of proportion to the circumstances. Perhaps, within herself was a deeply repressed thief from her childhood. The villain was the part of herself she failed or refused to acknowledge. Certainly there could have been a wide assortment of reasons for her behavior, but she was punishing the child not out of his need for correction but her own unconscious needs.

CUSTODY

The final tool our shadow uses to seek our attention is what we call *custody*. This tool seems to be the ultimate weapon of the unconscious. When all else has failed to gain our consideration, it seems the psyche has one last "big gun." In this final approach we find ourselves in the "grips" of a part of ourselves we have denied. Suddenly we are behaving in a way which seems completely incongruous with our normal personality. If we normally act with compassion and seek harmony, and then find ourselves acting ruthlessly and combatively with no regard for the consequences of our action, we may ask ourselves, "Where did that come from?" Or someone might tell us we were not acting at all like ourselves.

Jung put it this way:

The way in which complexes [shadow], "have us" is that the ego falls into a partial or total state of identity with them. There is no conscious separation between the ego and the impulsive, automatic energy drive of the complex. Hence there is no awareness of the complex as a separately existing entity. It is unconscious and there is no differentiation between ego motivations and the driving elements of the complex.[4]

When we are in the custody of our shadow we may use the old Flip Wilson line that "the devil made me do it." With this tool in control, we no longer "have" our shadow, rather, our shadow "has us." It needs our attention and in fact uses the most lethal weapon in its arsenal.

For myself, Bob, I find this occasionally when I am pushed to my limit. By nature, I am a strong personality, but very non-combative. I will be firm, but will avoid an argument. There are rare occasions when I will verbally attack someone without what I later feel is adequate provocation. When I do attack, I am ruthless. If someone in a store should provoke me, I can embarrass everyone around. Carol Ann simply leaves. Later, after I have calmed down, it is almost as if another person was acting. I seemed to be out of control, my shadow was in *custody*. Fortunately, these occasions are rare indeed, but when they do occur, my unconscious is using its ultimate weapon to signal my attention. Within me there is a raging Bob. One who requires acknowledgment and nurturing. A part of me which I am, at the time, ignoring.

A woman once told a story of sitting on a high bank next to a river with her grandson. Suddenly she was overwhelmed with an urge to throw the child into the river. She was horrified. She picked up the youngster, ran back to her car, and cried. Quite naturally, she was terribly distraught and frightened by the temptation. When we discussed the incident, we were able to point out the presence within each of us of a murderer.

Many of us can recall a time when we were so angry or distraught at someone or about something, that we discovered, to our horror, that we could kill. Indeed, each of us needs to have a healthy respect for that capacity within us. This woman had her shadow take her in its grips. Newspapers are daily full of stories of those who are in custody of their murderer or other parts of their shadow.

PROJECTIONS AND FREE WILL

While projections and custody can be extremely helpful in showing us our shadow side, if we fail to learn from them and integrate the characteristics to which they point, they can become increasingly destructive. When we are either projecting or in the shadow's custody, we are not exercising God's gift of free will over our behavior. Recall in chapter 4 when we spoke of the ego. We spoke of it as the residence of one of God's supreme gifts to the human being — free will. Surely, without free will, we could make no decisions. We could decide neither to accept nor reject God. Thus this is the ultimate spiritual tool given to us by God to separate us from all of God's other creatures.

When we are projecting our shadow or hidden selves on others, our resultant behavior and attitude toward those people is not an act of the ego and thus not fruit of our free will. When we see others through our projections, we have a distorted view of them. We cannot see them in truth as they really are, but only through our own weaknesses. To love others means to listen to them, to be present to them, to nurture them. When we look at other people — spouse, co-worker or anyone at all — and see not their true selves but our own hidden junk, we are not free to love them. We are acting out of our own need and not truly relating to them on the level of an honest relationship. How can true intimacy happen in any relationship when we are acting out of our unfreedom?

VICTIMS OF PROJECTIONS

When loved ones project on us, we have to respond to them through the maze of their own brokenness, we cannot be ourselves to them. The demands of their "stuff" prevent us from being authentic. Whether the victim of a positive or negative projection, when someone demands that we be other than our true selves, we are not free to be ourselves, free to be authentic. If, while we are in midlife, someone is projecting his or her midlife shadow on us, we find ourselves in the worst of situations.

OTHER TARGETS OF PROJECTIONS

Other victims of projections are *groups of people*. We project our individual and collective shadows on nations, races and religions. What we deny in ourselves, we project on Russians, or Chinese or blacks or Baptists or Catholics or Moslems or conservatives or liberals or Democrats or Republicans or Communists or Italians or Poles or women or men or teenagers or whomever! Wars begin when the collective shadows of nations are pitted against one another. Propagandists who understand this dynamic know how to whip countries into a frenzy with the proper rhetoric. During World War II, Germans and other Europeans projected their collective shadows on the Jews and the result was the Holocaust.

CUSTODY AND FREEDOM

Likewise, when our shadow has us, when we are in the custody of it, we are acting without freedom. As such, we are simply doing what comes naturally like the rest of the animal kingdom. We are not acting in freedom; we are acting compulsively. Compulsivity is the *opposite of freedom*. One of the roles of society and civilization is to insure its citizens do not behave like animals. There is a price for allowing ourselves to be in the grips of our shadow. One who simply "lets it all hang out" is likely to pay society's price. The price can be paid in social exclusion, a bad reputation, or jail. Laws are one of the preventions civilization uses to protect us from one another's shadows.

INTEGRATING THE SHADOW

It is clear that we cannot go around hanging our projections on loved ones and other individuals or groups, and we cannot allow ourselves the luxury of "doing what comes naturally" when the shadow beckons, but what can one do when it discovers the material we have long repressed into our unconscious? Let us look at the overall call of the midlife shadow.

Discovering hidden parts of ourselves is only the beginning of the midlife journey. Discovering what is inside does not authorize us to begin acting upon these hidden parts of ourselves.

Take the example of Anthony mentioned above. Were Anthony to recognize the hidden presence of his Don Juan, would he than be called to act upon this energy? Would he begin to dwell on possible fantasies? Certainly not. But given the progressive nature of the shadow's tools to deal with one who is not giving heed to its contents at midlife, we can speculate on some future scenario or temptation that could arise in Anthony's life. At present he is being assaulted by projections, but there could come a time when he might be attacked by a full-blown *custody situation*. In these situations, the Anthonys of the world find themselves unanswerably involved in situations they cannot imagine themselves. We are well advised to heed the psyche's early warnings!

But, if we are not called to act upon the shadow, just what is the call? Recall that in and of themselves, the contents of our shadow are amoral, neither good nor bad. They become evil when we fail to deal with them, when we continue to hang them on others or "do what comes naturally." The ego is the resident of God's gift of free will. Thus it is with the strength of the ego that we exercise morality and judgment upon our actions. When our behavior is determined by our shadow because we have failed to recognize hidden parts of ourselves, we fail to apply the gift of our learned morality and social values. Even the darkest part of our shadow can teach us something. We are called to recognize our hidden parts, acknowledge them, bow to them, integrate them. It is in our denying them that they gain their power over us. We are called to understand and take responsibility for having repressed these ideas, temptations, and fantasies and simply bring them into consciousness.

We must be willing to say "Yes, you are a part of me. (You, Don Juan. You, Murderer, You,...) You are within me, and I am no longer going to deny you. I will even give you a little space in me so I will know you better. But you are not going to control me." If done sincerely, over time, with valid recognition to match our words, this is good enough for the shadow. We must sometimes be willing to be firm with contents of the shadow. They will deny their existence, they will maintain they are not a problem. Yet we are in charge. We (our ego) must make decisions on our behavior and personality. By learning to recognize what the parts of the shadow *feel like*, we begin to know how to recognize them when they surface in the future. When they are recognized, when they are brought to consciousness, they lose their power to control us. We regain the God-given gift of FREEDOM.

And freedom is the preeminent gift of God. To act in freedom means that I am not driven. I choose my behavior. As said earlier, compulsivity is the opposite of freedom. When we are free to choose how we will act, to see others in truth and respond accordingly, we are acting with all our God-given attributes.

To *choose* means we have the opportunity to apply the Gospel values to our actions. We can ask ourselves if our behavior is the most appropriate behavior according to the circumstances, according to the Gospel value to love one another, according to God's Will for me at this time of my life. This is the stuff of free choices. This is the spiritual freedom that comes from intimacy with ourselves. By knowing the hidden parts of ourselves, we become strong and then, with God's continued grace, we build on that freedom and in our intimacy with others and God!

EVIL AND ORIGINAL SIN

Discovering the hidden self of which Paul speaks in Ephesians 3:14ff. is the reason that our midlife journey is a call to wholeness. The wholeness is found in discovering the many hidden treasures and dangers which become so stubbornly evident at midlife.

It is here that we would like to return to the idea of original sin and the concept of evil in relation to the model of the psyche we are using in this book. In chapter 4 when we offered the structure of the psyche, we identified the Self or God's Will at the core of our psyche. What then is our fallen nature or original sin? Where is the evil that we find so real within? By no means do we take these issues lightly, nor should anyone who chooses to make this midlife journey. We are each tempted toward evil. There is a self-centered magnetic force within each of us against which we must be constantly vigilant and pray for the grace to resist.

While we run the risk of again oversimplifying, sin as we know it is the opposite of love. Love is "other-centeredness" and sin is "self-centeredness." As our model clearly exhibits, within us we find both. Unfortunately, it seems self-centeredness often obscures our other-centeredness. We must wade through our sinful nature to discover God's Will for us. We must encounter the "junk" before we can find the "pearl of great price." Within, we find our sinful nature and evil incarnate. In her classic work *The Interior Castle*, St. Teresa of Avila makes it clear that when one travels inward, one must expect to meet the "serpents, vipers, and poisonous creatures." St. Ignatius of Loyola called the temptations which obscure God's Will "inordinate attachments," which had to be controlled before one could hear God's Will.

The journey of midlife is not for the fainthearted. Nor is it to be taken lightly. It is not one for which we are assured successful passage as we will see in the final chapter. When we confront our own brokenness and sinfulness, perhaps as never before, we run the risk of moral collapse. We can become overwhelmed by what we find. We can quickly abandon the journey as too painful and frightening, and we can yield to the lure of sin and find ourselves permanently in its grasp.

Within us we find both good and evil. But God assures us we will not be tempted beyond our strength. Perhaps we can see that our shadow is indeed part of the evil we find within and that God desires for us dominion over the tempter.

A good man [woman], draws what is good from the store of goodness in his [her] heart; a bad man [woman] draws what is bad from the store of badness. [Luke 6:45]

QUESTION FOR PERSONAL REFLECTION AND SMALL-GROUP SHARING

Suggested Scripture: Psalm 139:13–15

> *You created my inmost self,*
> *knit me together in my mother's womb.*
> *For so many marvels I thank you;*
> *a wonder am I, and all your works are wonders.*
> *You know me through and through,*
> *my being held no secrets from you,*
> *when I was being formed in secret,*
> *textured in the depths of the earth.*

PERSONAL PRAYER AND REFLECTION
PRELIMINARY NOTE

Begin this time of prayer by thanking the Lord for the gift of life, for your personality, for the way God has created you and loves you into life each day.

1. God has created us body, mind, and spirit. As we grow in understanding of our unconscious self, we also grow in spiritual and personal freedom, intimacy with ourselves, others, and God. This inner journey can only be undertaken with the help and grace of Jesus. While prayerfully reflecting on others in your life, find the one or two characteristics and idiosyncrasies in other people that most annoy you.

Then bring Jesus to mind as vividly as you are able. Ask him to gently and lovingly allow you to see these same characteristics operative in yourself. Perhaps you will discover these same traits in much different ways than you see them in others.

Next, look closely at this tendency or behavior in yourself. How does it surface? What stimulates you to use it or behave with it? How does it affect others? Is it connected with one of your gifts?

Finally, thank Jesus for the grace to be able to see this hidden part of ourselves and close this time of prayer.

Note: It is particularly helpful to write out this experience of prayer when it is complete. In addition, you may need to return to this a number of times and to share the experience with another person.

2. While prayerfully reflecting on others in your life, find the one or two characteristics and idiosyncrasies in other people that are most attractive to you.

Then bring Jesus to mind as vividly as you are able. Ask him to gently and lovingly allow you to see these same qualities operative in yourself. Perhaps you will discover these same gifts in much different ways than you see them in others.

Next, look closely at this tendency or behavior in yourself. How does it surface? What stimulates you to use it or behave with it? How does it affect others?

Finally, thank Jesus for the grace to be able to see this hidden gift within yourself and close this time of prayer.

SMALL-GROUP-SHARING QUESTIONS

1. Make a list of the characteristics and idiosyncrasies in other people that most annoy you. Number them in the order that they are most irritating.

Try to identify how those same characteristics may be present in your own life, perhaps wrapped in a much different cloak of circumstances. Remember, these characteristics are quite unconscious, thus are difficult to see. For some they will manifest themselves as temptations.

Share something you discovered about yourself.

2. *Make a list of the qualities and characteristics you most admire in others. Number them in the order that they are most attractive.*

Try to identify how those same characteristics may be present in your own life. Remember, these characteristics are quite unconscious, thus are difficult to see as well.

Share something you discovered about yourself.

3. *What are the characteristics you most strongly deny within yourself? Try to identify how those same characteristics may be present in your life.*

Share something you discovered about yourself.

Special note on questions 1, 2, and 3: This is one of the most difficult reflections in this book. Our natural tendency is to adamantly deny we could possess any of the characteristics that so repulse us in others or which attract us to others. This is natural. Nonetheless, if we seek God's grace, we can discover how these projections are, indeed, reflections of ourselves in some way.

8

Reintegration and Midlife

The final stage of the midlife transition is known as *reintegration*. It is the actual movement from the state of liminality or "in betweenness" to the second half of life. Reintegration is a time when some of the ambiguities and areas of gray encountered in the separation and liminality stages begin to clarify for us. Or, if they do not clarify, we at least decide we may be able to live with them.

ACCEPTING OUR LIMITATIONS

An important component of reintegration is acceptance of our own limitations. We begin to realize that we don't have to be everything for everyone. We may come to grips with our inability to meet expectations others place on us and in so doing we realize that it is okay and not really our problem.

This recognition of not meeting others' expectations can be an exceptionally freeing experience. It can feel like removing a heavy onus from our shoulders. Oftentimes trying to meet others' expectations is a hardship we don't even realize we are carrying or that we have carried it for a good part of our life. At reintegration we may begin to shed some of the weight of those expectations. We come to realize we are not the perfect person, wife, mother, parent, or friend, and never will be — but it's okay.

We Christians sometimes have the misconception that we need to be everything for everyone. Striving for perfection in all we do and all we are will lead us to a dead end. When at midlife we come face to face with our limitations, imperfections and shortcomings, we can choose to either deny them or accept them. When we accept our limitations, we usually find we will be more accepting also of others' limitations and shortcomings.

We once came in contact with a woman who was constantly chiding herself for all of the mistakes she made and limitations and flaws she saw in herself. Charlotte was a very involved and active church member. She was the leader of many organizations and worked very hard at being a woman for others. When people would ask her to do something, or call with a problem, she felt she always had to respond and be there for them. When she was unable to meet their needs or be of assistance she would become terribly down on herself. Her own expectations of her abilities far exceeded what was sometimes physically or emotionally possible. Charlotte also had very high expectations of others and expected perfection from them as well. When they fell short, she found it difficult to understand.

Charlotte's case is not that unusual. But during midlife we often have the opportunity to come face to face with our limitations and our poverty. As we understand our shortcomings, we are often more accepting and understanding of others as well.

This stage of reintegration is a time when we more consciously comprehend there are things we cannot do and qualities we do not have, and that it is okay. This realization is indeed a moment of spiritual growth for each of us. Thomas Merton tells us spiritual maturity is accepting our limitations joyfully.

For further reading on this topic, we recommend John Powell's *Happiness Is an Inside Job.*[1]

INTEGRATE OPPOSITES

Another facet of the reintegration stage of midlife is to begin to integrate the myriad of opposites which are found within us, to accept the paradox of our very existence. We can grow increasingly aware that we are both saint and sinner. We are capable of deep love and yet there are times when we are very selfish. Within us lies a deep creativity as well as an innate destructiveness. As we understand and accept these internal paradoxes we can grow in our freedom to nurture and use each as they are appropriate, to recognize when we are in the grips of our shadow and to move against it. Or, to use the gift of an "instant of pause" before we act; to determine if we are acting compulsively and if so, to ask if our behavior is appropriate. Is it appropriate to these circumstances, appropriate to the gospel values by which I profess to live, appropriate to God's will for me? This is the substance of which freedom is made.

With an acceptance of the paradox of opposites comes a sense of humility. As such, we may begin to acknowledge more clearly our gifts and at the same time recognize that our greatest gift can also be our point of weakness. Take, for example, people who have the gift of living in the present, that is, being very aware of all that is going on around them at any given moment and not worrying about the future. These people (termed sensors in Myers-Briggs parlance) are occasionally so present-oriented that they are unable to plan for the future or overlook the obstacles of the present to see the possibilities inherent in a situation.

We can become more aware of our weaknesses and even become thankful for those areas of our life. As we meditate on our lack of wholeness we may come to some new insights concerning our need for God. In our frailty and weakness we recognize Jesus as our strength and savior. We feel exceedingly grateful that his love continues even when our response is vacillating. We may come to learn that his love is greater than our sinfulness. This ambiguity of being broken yet thankful brings us to growth in a stance of extreme humility. Consequently we can begin to love and accept others in a deeper and less judgmental way because we see our own neediness.

Do not judge, and you will not be judged; because the judgements you give are the judgements you will get, and the standard you use will be the standard used for you. [Matthew 7:1–5]

CLEARER SENSE OF PURPOSE

As we reach toward reintegration we begin to have a clearer sense of purpose for our life. As we acquire this new found purpose it takes on the characteristics of a "mission" rather than a goal or dream. We begin to realize we don't need to conquer the world. We may see our mission in life to be a listener to the lonely, to visit the sick, or simply to be present to our family. We begin to realize that God is most present with us in the simplicity and routine of our everyday life of loving and being with others. The things we accomplish don't necessarily have to be grand and wonderful, but it is our faithfulness to the ordinary that is most important.

As we recall our life history, including the story of how God has been present in our lives, we may begin to see a pattern. How has God been present in our past in the times of deepest struggle and pain and in the times of hope and joy? How have we been touched and brought into wholeness and healing? Is there a pattern in my past experiences? When does the Lord Jesus seem to be most present to me? Is there a kind of repetition in these encounters? As we recollect our life history we may come to a clarity about our sense of mission. Often God will make us available to others as instruments of healing in areas where we have been deeply transformed through our life experience of pain, evil, and sin.

During reintegration we discover our mission because, if we have done the work of liminality, we have gone within and discovered our true and authentic identity. We have discovered at the core of our being God's Will for us. Indeed, this is the conversion of midlife. In our second half of life we may do nothing differently from what we did in the first half, but, if we have accomplished the labor of midlife, in our second half we will do what we do, not because it will please someone or because we need to make a mark in the world, but because we have discovered God's Will for us and have chosen to make that will our mission in life!

GENERATIVITY

Another side of that freedom which is found as we fully move into the second half of life is *generativity*. Generativity points to the willingness to use our power responsibly in the service and interest that goes beyond ourselves. It entails our concern for the world that will outlive us. Generativity is unselfish devotion to the well-being of others. It is an invitation to foster life and to continue to invest ourselves. Thus our involvement is guided less by our own needs and more by God's Will.

To accomplish this, we need to know ourselves, to be aware of our own psychological resources, our past and present social experience, what motivates us and when to hold on and when to let go. Many of these capabilities are learned as components of the midlife process. As such, it is a time to reflect on self-intimacy, our desire to exercise our talents in service of the community, and a progressive intimacy with God. Failure to respond to this stage of growth can render us passive, dormant, and stagnant in our personal as well as religious lives.

ACCEPT RESPONSIBILITY

As we strive toward reintegration at midlife we come face to face with the need for accepting responsibility for our own happiness. Have we blamed other people for our unhappiness or our afflictions in life? Have we ever said to ourselves, "My life would have been more worthwhile if only my spouse, parents, or friends had treated me differently?" Each of us is responsible for his or her own life. No one else can take that responsibility for us. No matter what our past life entailed, blaming others is not the answer for maturity at midlife. We may need to work through feelings of anger and guilt. We need to take responsibility for how we live our lives and the choices we make. No one else can be held accountable for our choices except us.

Today we are becoming increasingly aware of the number of us who grew up in dysfunctional families. They may have been dysfunctional because of alcohol or drug abuse. We may have been physically, emotionally, or sexually abused or lived in an atmosphere of compulsive behavior which had and continues to have a debilitating effect on us. We are each the product of our early environment and we adopt many of the dysfunctional traits of our family. We have also learned that we tend to make ourselves responsible for the dysfunction of our parents and family members.

At midlife, we often come face to face with these inherited traits and we are invited to be healed by taking responsibility for our behavior and our lives. As we grow in this area we become increasingly able to let go of the sense that we were the cause of the turmoil in our family.

I, Carol Ann, can see how this was played out in my own life. As I recall patterns of my childhood I remember how quiet and mild I was as a child. There was tension in my family as I was growing up, and I wanted very much to avoid being a burden on anyone. As I reflect on this time of my life I see the responsibility I accepted for the well-being of my family. I believed that if I behaved and was good it might have a positive effect on how the rest of the family was doing. Thus I worked very hard at being well behaved. I tried to say the right things and do what was expected of me. I wanted to please everyone.

Through looking at these patterns in my life I see how I have taken a responsibility for many people and circumstances that has been inappropriate. It has taken patience and insight on my part to see how these old patterns sometimes affect my life today. I have had to learn that when my children do something of which I would not approve, I am not responsible. When they make decisions differently than I, I am not responsible for their choices. When Bob has different opinions or acts in ways I may not think appropriate, I allow the problem to be his. These might seem obvious now, but many times this sense of responsibility is on an unconscious level and does deeply affect our behavior. Through prayer, journaling, and regular meetings with a spiritual director, I have been able to be more aware of my emotions and my feeling responsible for meeting others' inappropriate expectations.

It is vital that we take steps to grow in these areas as they affect all aspects of our lives: our self-image, our relationships with our spouse, our children, others, and with God. There are numerous programs available today which recognize this pattern and offer valuable help in the healing process. Twelve-step programs, including Al-Anon and Adult Children of Alcoholics, are but a few. We strongly recommend *Bradshaw on: The Family* by John Bradshaw which deals head on with many of these issues.[2]

INTEGRITY

Reintegration should bring about integrity. Integrity is the challenge of the developmental task of affirming the meaning of life. It is in the realization that the expected and the unexpected happenings of my life are all vitally related to who I am now. There is an embracing of my life passages as well as those people who have been significant in my life. This self-acceptance brings about freedom, wholeness, and reintegration as we move into the second half of life. It is through the psychological resources of integrity that we are able to distinguish the meaning of our own life, even with all its ambiguities and uncertainties. If accomplished, we can live by our inner values and not by what other people will say or think about us. Part of discovering God's Will for us is to get in touch with those inner values and begin to make the decisions and, if necessary, the changes to live by them.

FORGIVENESS

Finally, an authentic movement into the second half of life requires a time of forgiveness. This may be forgiveness of ourselves, other people in our lives, or perhaps even God. Indeed, one of the most significant barriers we can encounter to facilitating a successful midlife transition may be our unwillingness to forgive. As we carry the pain of past hurts into our later years, they can wither the creative energy and joy we are meant to experience.

Much of our psychological and spiritual growth is related to forgiveness. This forgiveness very often is pointed toward our parents. If only my parents had been different. They can become scapegoats and we may blame *them* instead of taking responsibility for our own life. Forgiveness and acceptance of them are often a turning point in midlife.

We often learn patterns of dealing with other people, including family members. I know for me, Bob, lack of forgiveness has some deep roots in my own history. I grew up in a neighborhood surrounded by relatives. Nearly all of my father's brothers and sisters lived in our small country neighborhood at one time or another. Our house was one house off the road; to reach it we had to drive past the house owned by my father's twin brother and his family. One of my best friends growing up was a cousin, George, who lived in that house. For my entire life, I don't recall my parents or George's parents ever speaking a word to one another! There had been deep hurts prior to George's and my birth, but they were never really healed, and now all but one of those parents are dead. In reflecting on that strange but all too common phenomenon, I realized that I have to work hard at breaking that pattern of unforgiveness that I learned through much of my upbringing. Today, when I am tempted to get angry at a family member, I must bring that pattern to mind and counter it with a spirit of love and forgiveness.

Many of us come from families or know of families who have been alienated from one another for years without even knowing the reason. Sometimes we can initiate a change in these relationships and sometimes not, but we can have a change of attitude and heart. With God's grace and help we can forgive ourselves and others. Our Church offers the Sacrament of Reconciliation as an instrument of the love and forgiveness of our Father.

Sometimes our wounds may be so deep that we may need psychological counseling or therapy as a vehicle to guide us in our midlife transition. It takes courage to enter into a counseling relationship, but many will attest to this being a most beneficial and healing step on the midlife journey.

Our individual past often remains relatively hidden or forgotten because it holds our own failures and unforgiven transgressions. We are invited at midlife to allow those past wounds to be healed and forgiven. As we invoke the Lord to show us areas of our past and present that need forgiveness and healing, those prospective wounds may come to our attention. *Healing of Memories* by Dennis and Matthew Linn address this topic with concrete avenues of healing and forgiveness through prayer.[3]

AUTHENTIC IDENTITY

We have used the word *identity* throughout all three of the stages of midlife. In reintegration we will examine the meaning of the term *authentic identity*. Finding our authentic identity takes time, prayer, and partaking in the inner journey. St. Teresa of Avila in *The Interior Castle* describes her journey to God in prayer.[4] She speaks time and time again of the importance of self-knowledge on this journey to the center of the castle where God dwells and to a divine union. As we progress and grow in our prayer and in our relationship with God, we go through many different stages but each one entails a growing aspect of self-knowledge. As we get closer to our center, which is God, we become more understanding of our own unique and authentic identity.

Self-knowledge and our authentic identity go hand in hand. We do not discover our identity alone; it is not something private but is accomplished in the context of our community, our spouse, children, and friends. Each of our in-depth relationships help us to know ourselves better. We need one another for support, encouragement, and intimate relationships that can nurture and assist us in this midlife journey.

As we move through the different stages of midlife transition and our inner journey, we have the opportunity to grow in understanding of our true self. We become more aware of a need to cease identifying solely with our occupations and roles, our possessions or talents. Rather, we discover the deeper picture of who we are in God's eyes. It is a time when we long for the full adventure of life and desire to find out who we truly are, why we were created.

If we pray and ask, we will receive the answer; if we search, we will find our authentic identity. If we knock, the door will be opened to us. Our true identity comes from God. We grow in that knowledge by belief and faith. Only with the kind of belief that comes from our heart and spirit do we find we are truly a son or daughter of God. As we believe, live, and pray from that identity as Child of God, we will discover our authentic identity as we move forward in the second half of life.

THE TASK OF REINTEGRATION — INTIMACY WITH GOD

The task of this final stage of midlife is to develop intimacy with our God. Dealing with all of the above is an extraordinary part of developing that intimacy. Reintegration is a sacred time, a chance to encounter God with a deeper trust and vulnerability. God is a God of now, of the present moment. We can move into the second half of our lives with that profound awareness. It is God's invitation to us. "Be still and know that I am God" (Psalm 46:10).

This invitation should lead us to prayer and meditative reflection and an increased attention to our inner life. It may be a time when we come into a more contemplative prayer life. We may use fewer words and be more attentive to listening for the Lord in the silence. In this prayer of quiet, ego activity is minimal. We can nurture an outer and inner stillness with a loving openness to God. This intimacy with God also comes with an increased awareness of God's action in our everyday life.

Even when we have had an intimate relationship with God our whole life long, there is still more. He has His hand outstretched to us at this stage of our life because it is such an important time of growth psychologically as well as spiritually. Growth and change don't happen automatically. We need the help and grace of Jesus as our companion and our guide. As we pray with the scriptures and allow the words of the Lord to be personal for us in our life today and allow those words to heal us and to call us to grow and change and come to an acceptance of our life, we will be responding to the call to intimacy with the Lord.

Midlife is an invitation, but not one we automatically accept. It is our choice whether we respond to this invitation. It takes courage and maturity to be willing to open ourselves to God at this time of midlife.

It is often embarrassing and unexpected to be caught in an upheaval of our inner and outer worlds. We expect ourselves to be stable and mature. We may often attempt to disguise the passage of midlife from ourselves, others, and even God. When this occurs, religious stagnation can result. We tend to hold on rather than to give ourselves away. We can become very rigid and unwavering in a dormant and passive kind of way. We may become closed and put up barriers in our relationship with God and with others.

This entire process concerns individuation. It is through the process of individuation that we come to a renewed wholeness and vigor about life. Yet, as we see, individuation is a deeply spiritual experience. It is here we can recall Jung's observation that he never saw anyone healed, that is, he never saw anyone have a successful midlife transition who didn't get in touch with his or her God.

While we may choose to accept the invitation to intimacy with God and with ourselves and others, it may not be a smooth road. But it will be one in which new energies may come alive in us, new hope and freedom. We may become aware of new resources in quiet and solitude. These shifts can make us more available to others in that we are less driven by our own selfish desires, and make us more available to the community and others in new ways, using resources and potential we are yet discovering.

QUESTION FOR PERSONAL REFLECTION AND SMALL-GROUP SHARING

Suggested Scripture: Luke 11:9, 10

So I say to you: "Ask, and it will be given to you; search, and you will find: knock, and the door will be opened to you. For everyone who asks receives; everyone who searches finds; everyone who knocks will have the door opened."

PERSONAL PRAYER AND REFLECTION
PRELIMINARY NOTE

Ask God your Father, in the name of the Son and through the working of the Holy Spirit to fill your whole being with a deep trust in himself as Lord.

1. Bring to mind how God has been present in your life history. Become aware of your past experiences and how God has touched you and healed you. Take some time to allow these experiences to surface.
A. Does God deal with you according to some pattern?
B. When is Jesus most present to you?

2. (You will need your Bible for this reflection.) Forgiveness is a central issue of midlife. With God's help, bring to mind a person who has hurt or disappointed you whom you may not have fully forgiven. Briefly recall what happened between you. In your imagination, with the help and grace of Jesus, forgive that person and ask for forgiveness for the times you hurt or disappointed him or her.
Finally, read Psalm 103 (He forgives all your offenses), Luke 15:11–32 (the prodigal son), or Luke 23:33–34 (forgive them Father, . . .). Allow the words of the scripture to touch your heart.

Take your time with this prayer even if it requires returning to it several different times for prayerful reflection.

SMALL-GROUP-SHARING QUESTIONS

1. A significant characteristic of the reintegration stage of midlife is accepting our gifts as well as our limitations. Of which gifts and limitations am I becoming more aware as I enter this stage. How do I feel about this?

2. After reflecting on my past history and better knowing my gifts and limitations, is a clearer sense of mission emerging for the second half of my life? Describe that mission as best you can and share how you might nurture it and bring it to generativity (serving the broader world and generations to come).

3. Are there people in my life whom I have not forgiven? Do I need to forgive myself? Do I hold any anger toward God? How might this be a barrier to my personal and spiritual growth?

4. Do I find today I am more able to live by my own inner values and less by what others might think or say of me? If so, share a little of how I am doing this and how it makes me feel.

5. My true and authentic identity comes from knowing and believing I am a son or daughter of God. Am I more able to believe, live, and pray from this perspective? What must I do to foster this type of intimacy with God?

9

The Other Man and Woman at Midlife

We knew this chapter title would be provocative. We knew also that it would tap into the all too frequent midlife experience of a heightened attraction to the opposite sex and sexual affairs. In our ministry we are constantly confronted by spouses with stories of mates who have suddenly taken on a lover after twenty to thirty years of seeming fidelity.

On the less dramatic side, at midlife we may find ourselves with renewed sexual fantasies and dreams which we thought were put to rest when we moved from adolescence to adulthood. Perhaps we find ourselves now sexually aroused by a person who has been a long-time platonic friend and find ourselves embarrassed and upset.

By understanding the hidden man and woman within us, we may be able to withstand some of these distressing storms of midlife and, in fact, advance the process toward a constructive rather than destructive outcome. When speaking of the *hidden man* or *woman* within us, we speak of the very real presence of a contrasexual element deep within each of our psyches.

Before elaborating on this hidden man and woman within us, let us first focus upon the *dominant* structural forms of the feminine and masculine psyche. They are discussed in a very fine book *About Men and Women* by Tad and Noreen Guzie.[1]

Within the psyche each man establishes a dominant masculine identity, known as his masculine archetype, that will comprise the essence of his personality. Likewise, each woman has a dominant feminine archetype that will have a strong effect on her personality.

FEMININE ARCHETYPES

There are four basic feminine archetypes. By no means are they all inclusive, but they can be used as a starting point. They are *Mother, Companion, Amazon*, and the *Medium*. On a diagram, they appear as follows:

Each of these four basic archetypes carries both a positive and negative side. Normally a woman relates strongly to one of these archetypes for the first half of her life and at midlife begins to draw upon a second. As we grow in maturity, we should be able to identify to a small extent with *each* of the archetypes. The main thrust for this theory comes from Toni Wolff, a longtime associate of Jung, in her *Structural Forms of the Feminine Psyche*.[2]

The Mother

The woman who identifies with the Mother archetype usually encounters her identity and finds life fulfillment in nurturing, protecting, and the maternal instinct. This is the archetype which historically is most strongly supported by our society and the one to which women most relate. The Mother is one who has a collective orientation toward others. Her sense of helping and supporting those who need assistance is a strong part of her makeup. She is attracted to situations where she is needed by others.

The archetypal Mother who does not marry will likely have a profession with a maternal role such as nursing, social work, teaching, or homemaking. She will be drawn to a career where she can use those attributes of nurturing and caring for others. If she chooses marriage, the Mother will be interested in the social status of her husband in his career and in society. His position in the world is of utmost importance to her. Mothers often refer to their husbands as "Dad" or "Father" in conversations with others as well as with him.

Negative Mother

There is a dark side to each of the archetypes as well. This dark side can present itself in either of two extremes: when it is denied or when it is affirmed to the exclusion of the other archetypes. We will discuss this further on.

When the dark side of the Mother appears, she blocks out the positive and life-giving qualities and exhibits the opposite characteristics. These negative aspects of the Mother take the positive nourishing and caring qualities and turn them to a smothering attitude. She will mother when it is not appropriate and her mothering will take on a devouring quality. She will want to mother everyone even when it is not appropriate. For this reason the Mother may have more difficulty at midlife letting go of her grown children. She may also have a tendency to smother her grandchildren with an unhealthy controlling love. The negative expression of the Mother is a camouflage for one who is dependent and insecure and may feel quite powerless.

The Companion

The feminine archetype of Companion (often known as Hetaira or Puella) is the woman who finds her meaning in warm, personal relationships. On our diagram above, you will notice she is opposite the Mother archetype. She may *companion* others intellectually, emotionally, spiritually, or sexually. She usually has a youthful spontaneity about her.

The Companion draws love out of others and she usually conveys a radiance. She has a very individual and personal way of relating to others. Her relationships are quite important to her and she values communication and equality in them. She may find herself quite energized and inspired in her relationships. It is in these relationships that the Companion finds her identity. She tends to be free, loving, and trusting. She is usually instinctively related to the personal psychology of anyone she befriends. A Companion can help put a man in touch with his unconscious, and for the man fortunate enough to have a Companion as spouse or close friend, this may be especially helpful in the second half of life as he moves toward individuation.

Negative Companion

Let us look at the dark side of the Companion. If neglected or related to exclusively, the Companion may neglect her family and social obligations in favor of her all-important need for relationship. She may even set aside her own interests, activities, or personal values for the sake of companionship. The Companion may be both manipulative and demanding of others' time and attention. She may have a tendency to tease men, and countless times Companions have led to the breakup of marriages. When these negative qualities are present in the Companion, she will likely feel trapped, lonely, and in pain.

The Amazon Woman

The Amazon (sometimes known as Wonder Woman) finds her identity and fulfillment in managing the outer world and society. She is both intellectual, capable, and wholesomely ambitious. She has a tendency toward independence and is concerned with her own individual development. She will often be a career woman, although this is not always the case. She is often committed to an ideal or cause and usually has sufficient energy and drive not only to succeed in what she undertakes but to flourish and excel. The Amazon is usually drawn toward outer achievements. She is more dedicated to collective and impersonal values than she is toward people. In her relationships with men, she can be a stimulating colleague or friend who makes few demands.

The Negative Amazon

The dark side of the Amazon, which will surface when this archetype is either denied or related to singularly, is a woman who is frivolous and silly. She is one who playacts and is out to please. She may be out to show men she is better than they are and can both hound and haunt them. The negative Amazon may become so frustrated with her own outer expectations that she loses her true feminine identity. She may be overwhelmed with these expectations and become very angry with the men around her who are connected with them. Her dark ambition may be to be queen of all and will stomp on others who get in her way.

The Medium

The Medium woman is intuitive. Recall on our diagram, she is the opposite of the Amazon. She has a capacity to bridge the inner and the outer worlds, or the conscious and unconscious of herself and others. Her energy can balance an egocentric society. She may be a mystic, healer, prophetess, or poet. While not always apparent to herself, at the core of her being she has the capacity for both a rewarding imagination and oneness with God. She is immersed in the collective unconscious and needs to develop a strong ego to differentiate between the conscious and unconscious, the personal and impersonal, and the material and psychic. The Medium woman is usually not very public and she is the type least accepted in our culture. She may sense what is going on under the surface of a group. If she learns discernment, she may verbalize what is unseen and unconscious to others. This type of woman has an important role in mediating the world of the unconscious to men and can find herself assisting other people in dying, especially men.

The Negative Medium

The dark side of the Medium is cut off from the spiritual world and can be involved in the occult and superstition. She may find herself inundated with the inner world. She may be full of ideas and speculation but at the same time full of disturbance, confusion, and chaos. She may have a mysterious primitive passion and become inflated with her own seeming great authority. If she does not develop a strong ego, she can become a source of confusion to herself and others. On the dark side of the Medium, she is lost, lonely, cut off from God, and oblivious to outer reality.

As we have seen, each archetype has both light and dark sides. If we see our own archetype as the only way, we will likely experience its dark side. We need to recognize our basic story or archetype but also to realize that each of the others are positive and a part of our unconscious. Midlife is a time to discover and bring to consciousness one of the other archetypes for development and wholeness.

As with all of the feminine archetypes, it is helpful to see where our deepest story lies, but also to be in touch with the other three stories that are in our unconscious. Wholeness lies in accepting and holding the whole gift of God. We are indeed all four types, even though we may only consciously recognize one or two in ourselves. This journey to wholeness is a lifelong process. To deny any of our gifts or to fail to see the value in each would be to turn our back on the gift. If we deny any of these archetypes, it will turn negative for us.

THE MASCULINE ARCHETYPES

Just as there are four feminine archetypes which are in the forefront of feminine consciousness there are four masculine archetypes from which men will take their identity. The four masculine archetypes are the *Father, Eternal Boy*, the *Warrior* and the *Sage*. Using a similar diagram, these archetypes are displayed as follows:

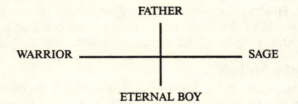

The Father

The masculine archetype of the Father is parallel to that of the Mother. The Father is a natural leader. He is often the protector and director of others. His nature is to safeguard and support his family or whoever is in his charge. He relates in a personal way to the collective form of functioning. While not always the case, very often the Father will marry. The Father tends to be conservative and strongly traditional. He values stability and the collective values passed down through the generations. The Father may call his wife "Mother" even long after the children have left home.

The Negative Father

When the dark side of the Father emerges, he may become a strict authoritarian and may be rigid and inflexible. He does not usually encourage independent thinking or new ways of doing things for himself and those in his charge. At midlife it is essential for the Father to look at other masculine archetypes to more fully develop and to become less one-sided.

The Eternal Boy

The Eternal Boy, often known as the Seeker or Puer Aeternus, is the direct opposite of the Father. The masculine Eternal Boy corresponds to the Companion in the feminine. The Eternal Boy seeks his own individuality and is always looking for new opportunities and experiences. He rarely concerns himself with permanence or authority. While the Father relates to others in a *collective way*, that is, as children, workers, politicians, the Eternal Boy relates to people in an *individual* way. His relationships are more one-on-one and intimate. Consequently, the Eternal Boy usually seeks one-on-one peer relationships with a variety of men and women. It is usually very easy to strike up a casual conversation with him. He is frequently off on new adventures and with new relationships. He is always seeking the new idea and new venture. He may bring exuberance and fresh new ideas to a situation. He may be upsetting to the Father type who is more concerned with stability and long-term relationships.

The Negative Eternal Boy

Should a man neglect the Eternal Boy or relate exclusively to this archetype, he will likely experience the negative or dark side. The dark side of the Eternal Boy is often seen as he seeks new ventures. He may risk his financial security for the sake of the opportunity. The immature seeker is irritated by any constraint placed on his independence. This man often never seems to grow up and can show signs of irresponsibility. Without self-discipline, the Eternal Boy will lack balance in his life. He may be inclined to blame others for his failures.

The Warrior

The following masculine archetype, the Warrior, corresponds to the feminine Amazon. The Warrior is sometimes known as the Hero. He relates to nonpersonal goals in a collective way. He enjoys competition and it often seems to bring out the very best in him. Warriors have a need for recognition of themselves and the things with which they are involved. Their energies are usually geared toward accomplishments, achievements, and conquering. The Warrior likes to manage power and to work with the power structure to execute his goals. Efficiency is a high concern and will sometimes be his priority over people. This archetype is the type of which our society most approves for men in their twenties and thirties.

The Negative Warrior

Most difficult for the Warrior is his dealing with people and their personal concerns and interests. Also, the Warrior should be careful with their use of power over other people. It is helpful for them to develop strong personal values and wisdom to keep their power in perspective. At midlife the Warrior will benefit from using some of his energy and drive for developing his inner world and goals and relating to the interior part of himself.

The Sage

The Sage, sometimes known as the Wise Man, is more interested in knowledge and one-on-one interaction than in competition and achievement like the Warrior or Father. The Sage is opposite the Warrior. He is drawn toward the inner world. His best interaction with others lies in sharing ideas and theories or visions. He is more idea oriented than people oriented. His inner drive is to place himself and others in touch with ideas worth considering. At his best the Sage is a prophet. The Sage's source of energy is in the search for the meaning of things. He often helps others to understand the significance of their experiences. He has an in-depth desire to search for conscious meaning and he will usually organize his world around philosophy.

The Negative Sage

The dark side of the Sage is his inability to accomplish things. For him, implementing all of his ideas in the outer world can be laborious and tedious. He may lack patience in dealing with practical detail. The immature Sage may become inflated with his own ideas. He may masquerade as the wise one but may be deluding himself with a wisdom he does not possess.

RELATING TO OUR ARCHETYPE

These eight archetypes of masculine and feminine structural forms are modes and variations that find expression in different individual personalities to varying degrees. They are symbolic representations of energies. Each of us as men and women possesses all four masculine or feminine structural forms as latent potentials. We will relate to one or possibly two in a conscious way. The structural forms to which we fail to relate may turn their negative side to us if they go completely unacknowledged. They become, as it were, part of our shadow, subject to all the tools of the shadow, including projections and being in custody. This is especially true of the archetype opposite our dominant archetype. This will frequently be our blind spot, but we can consider how all four forms are operative in our personalities and the stories of ourselves we relate to others. Your source of energy and the story that best explains your life and the most comfortable choices you make will help you determine your main archetypal energy.

Archetypes explain the source of our personal values. It is helpful to consider your own strengths in these areas of masculine or feminine energies. They are gifts to us from God.

THE *OTHER* MAN AND WOMAN

Within each woman, in addition to all of her dominant and conscious feminine qualities, lies what are often latent unconscious *masculine* characteristics, or what is known as *focused consciousness*. Here are found traits such as assertiveness, logos or word power, decisiveness, and protectiveness. The archetypal term for these more naturally inactive characteristics in a woman is know as her *Animus*.

While these traits are not exclusively masculine or the domain of the man, they indeed are historically and anthropologically more naturally found in the man's dominant personality. One could argue that they have become masculine because of a patriarchal cultural bias and are totally androgynous within the psyche. While we will leave this sensitive issue for another time, let us point out that cultural bias frequently develops as a result of archetypal energy within the human psyche, thus we come to the proverbial issue of the "chicken and the egg."

In the same way, the latent unconscious feminine components in a man's personality are known as the *Anima*. These are characteristics more naturally found in the women's dominant personality and include such qualities as diffuse awareness, relatedness, sensitivity, receptivity, compassion, and faithfulness.

As observed by C. G. Jung, these psychological phenomenon are facets of the shadow at a much deeper level than we have spoken of earlier. The Anima and Animus are at the deepest part of the shadow and in a structural sense could be said to surround the Self or God's Will. Thus these deep elements of our psyche shroud God's Will but also are closest to it and can tell us much about it.

Understanding the Anima/Animus concept can be of significant benefit during our midlife years. Jung maintained that the task of development in midlife lies in counterbalancing the one-sidedness of a person's earlier life or first half. For most of us, our contrasexual characteristics, or Anima/Animus, are not called upon during the first half of life. Yet, as midlife approaches, as a deep part of our shadow, they demand attention, recognition, and integration.

A heterosexual man will likely identify his ego with his masculinity and his feminine side remains quite unconscious to him. Likewise, a heterosexual woman most often identifies herself consciously with her femininity, and her masculine side remains similarly unconscious until her midlife years.

Rather than use our own latent contrasexual qualities, we unconsciously depend on others of the opposite sex, including our spouse, to act them out for us. At midlife the Anima or Animus within us, if unacknowledged, can cause lamentable complications in our relationships. John Sanford's *The Invisible Partners* deals with this issue in great detail.[3]

PROJECTING THE ANIMA/ANIMUS

The Anima and Animus, while deeper in the unconscious than other parts of the shadow, use the same tools mentioned in chapter 7 to gain our attention and integration at midlife. They make themselves known through our prayer and dreams. It is interesting to note that symbols of our Anima and Animus take the form of characters with our opposite sex. That is, when men dream of women, they are dreaming of their Anima. When a woman dreams of men, she is dreaming of her Animus. Dreams signal a part of the unconscious which is seeking integration. Thus attention to our dreams can serve us well in the midlife journey.

The Anima/Animus also use the tool of projection. We have a tendency to project onto others hidden or unacknowledged aspects of our personality. Any "negative" trait we fail to acknowledge in ourselves will be projected onto other persons and have a strong irritating effect upon us. Likewise, repressed "positive" characteristics will be projected, and we might be enamored of the target of our projection. Whenever any kind of projection occurs, the person who is the target of our unconscious projection is either greatly overvalued or greatly undervalued. In other words, we are powerfully attracted to them or repulsed by them. When the projection involves the Anima or Animus, the targets of our projections, both positive and negative, are usually members of the opposite sex.

Midlife is a time when our unconscious searches for integration. Our natural feminine or masculine tendencies call out for a balance of their opposites. If we choose to ignore this call to integration, we may find ourselves quite fascinated by someone of the opposite sex who personifies our own latent contrasexual characteristics. In *Invisible Partners*, John Sanford says it this way:

...whenever a man or woman fascinates us we can be sure that a projected content of the unconscious is at work. In their all-too-human reality people are not fascinating; it is the archetypal figures of the unconscious that are fascinating. Recognizing fascinating projections when they occur makes it possible for us to become aware of the anima/animus figures who stand behind these projections... the most common way for the anima to claim a man's attention is to fill his mind with a powerful sexual-erotic fantasy, and, similarly, it is the animus who lies behind many a woman's sexual-erotic fantasy about a man. It is as though the inner figures are trying in this way to get our attention.[4]

When this happens to us we can look at the qualities that most fascinate us in that person and ask, "How is that trait present within me?" We can ignore these attractions, or try to push them out of our mind, or feel embarrassed by them, or we can learn from them. We can ask for the Lord's help to find these qualities in ourselves. These qualities may be calling out to be developed and acknowledged.

An example of this would be a very feminine woman who is aware of many of her feminine qualities but not so much in touch with her masculine traits such as decisiveness or assertiveness, and her ability to voice her deep inner convictions to others. She may find these characteristics very attractive and even fascinating in the men she encounters. Likewise, a man who has been a very assertive and strong leader, and has never developed his more gentle receptive side may find himself attracted or even infatuated with a woman who exemplifies these latter traits. This may be his Anima's way of showing him traits that are calling for acknowledgment and development. If we don't understand what is happening we can be caught off guard and respond in inappropriate ways in our relationships with people of the opposite sex.

While this experience is exacerbated during midlife, it is forever active and, in fact, positive Anima/Animus projection is the source of most romantic love. If our positive Anima/Animus images are mutually projected between a man and woman at the same time, we have that seemingly perfect state of romantic infatuation. As these latent qualities demand our attention at midlife, our projections take on a renewed vigor and, if blatantly acted out rather than heeding the call for integration, we can find ourselves in rather ominous situations.

Midlife is a call to inner development and knowledge. This can be difficult to achieve and is very easily put off in deference to allowing another person to carry these contrasexual characteristics for us. For example, the very feminine woman we described above may have let her husband carry her masculine assertiveness through much of her adult life just as her father may have carried it for her as a child. Now, at midlife, her husband may be developing his own feminine traits and may no longer be willing or able to carry her share of masculinity. The wife has two choices here: she can begin to develop these characteristics for herself or she can unconsciously try to find another "hook" on whom to hang her projections and who will carry her masculinity for her once again. She may find this easy to do as she steps out into the work world or attends the local health club.

The exact same holds for a man whose mother and then wife have carried his Anima traits. Coincident with these traits becoming more active in him, his wife may be responding to the call of her masculine Animus traits and begin to reject his need for her to carry his nurturing, gentle Anima. He too has a choice: integrate or look for someone else to carry these traits. He may have no idea what he is looking for as he is suddenly attracted to a woman at work or the coffee shop or wherever. His sexual fantasies about this woman may also increase.

In both of these examples, which is all too common at midlife, the situations have the potential to ruin lives. Both the men and women would do well to look into themselves and discover how the qualities that most attract them to their new "fascination" exist within themselves. In order for them to nurture and develop these qualities in themselves they must first value them in others, both of the opposite, and of their same sex. They must believe these attributes are God-given gifts to themselves. To discover and develop these qualities the man and woman must let these traits become a part of their inner search, their inner journey. In reality it is much easier to see and be drawn to these traits in another all the while unconsciously believing they will fill the lack in their own developmental journey.

Integration is a slow process. It entails seeing and believing that these traits are within us, seeing the value and giftedness of these characteristics. This is not just an intellectual knowledge but a felt knowledge. It entails gradually developing and using these traits in our own life, not just valuing them in others.

Each individual must first be rooted in their own masculinity or femininity before they can develop the opposite characteristics. As we are grounded in who we are and accepting of our own valuable masculine or feminine gifts, we can then slowly integrate their opposites.

Do we women really value our femininity, the traits of gentleness, receptivity, sensitivity and tenderness? Do we men really value our gifts of assertiveness, decisiveness and protectiveness? Have we developed these gifts to their fullest potential? Two excellent books on the topic are *He, the Psychology of the Mas-*

culine[5] and *She, the Psychology of the Feminine*[6] both by Robert Johnson.

IN CUSTODY OF THE ANIMA/ANIMUS

The second way our Anima/Animus can deal with us is through what we call *custody*. As before, we may find ourselves in the grip of the negative Anima or Animus and not be able to understand what got into us. A man in the grip of his Anima may find himself overwhelmed by moods or taking a passive or cynical attitude toward life. A woman finding herself in the custody of her Animus might find herself inexplicably acting in an argumentative, dogmatic, and stubborn fashion.

INTEGRATION OF THE ANIMA/ANIMUS

Integration is an ever ongoing process in our life. We will never reach completion or wholeness until we are with God in heaven. We need to relate to our Anima and Animus in our inner world. But how do we do this? We briefly suggest some techniques here that we will elaborate in chapter 13. By using techniques of writing in a journal and dialogue with these hidden parts of ourselves we can begin to relate to them. For both men and women it is essential that they express their feelings to those close to them. Hiding our feelings or pushing them away allows for the negative side of our Anima or Animus to take hold and a man will be caught in his moodiness and a woman in her dogmatic assertiveness. A man needs to develop warm and meaningful human relationships where he can express his feelings.

For a woman to integrate her Animus, she needs to have fulfillment of her goals and aspirations. A woman can better understand her Animus by looking at the important men in her life as she was growing up, such as her father or the father figure. What were his values, what did he hold as important in life, what were his religious convictions and beliefs? The same is true for the man to look at the important woman in his life as he was growing up, especially his mother, and ask what was important in her, where did her value lie, what were her convictions about life, God, and relationships? If we can discover these things (or at least our perception of them) we will be uncovering aspects of our own masculinity and femininity.

There are both positive and negative attributes to these

archetypes, but it is relating to them and understanding them that moves us to a new freedom at midlife. A freedom which permits us not to be driven by what comes naturally, but to choose our behavior in freedom, to choose the way we will relate to other people. With God's grace, through prayer and discernment, and with a willingness on our part to work through the difficulties and pain, we can grow in intimacy with ourselves, others, and God. We can do so partially by growing in our understanding of both the masculine and feminine aspects of our unconscious as we bring them to light.

Just as the shadow in general can have a powerful effect on our lives at midlife, the Anima and Animus, if unintegrated can draw us into midlife decisions which can totally block the midlife experience and bring about an all too common failure. Failure at midlife will be discussed in detail in our closing chapter. Jung maintained that the integration of our Anima/Animus is intrinsic to success at midlife.

At the same time, by listening to our unconscious, we can integrate qualities which will bring a new sense of beauty and balance to our personalities, that will allow us to relate to our spouse and others in a new fullness of relationship. We can have a new sense of the statement in Genesis 1:27:

God created man in the image of himself, in the image of God he created him, male and female he created them.

10

Enriching Marriage
at Midlife

As we, Carol Ann and Bob, personally continue our journey
through midlife, we have found it to be the most rewarding and
hope-filled time of our lives. While it has also been a time of
disturbing inner stirrings and transformations, we are convinced
that for us, only with the grace of our Sacrament have we been
able to traverse this awesome experience with love and a deepening commitment to one another. We are further convinced
that this grace has included the God-given ability to communicate with one another with a deep trust and openness. From
this openness has come an intimacy we would have never imag-
ined possible, and this kind of intimacy can be the wonderful
fruit of the midlife transition. From the pain and suffering of
the cross, Jesus brought us new life in the resurrection. Out of
our own pain and suffering comes the hope of deepened love
and intimacy as God's invitation to us as a married couple.

INTIMACY IN MARRIAGE

Marital intimacy may have a different meaning to each one of
us. Our own definition of intimacy explores three levels: the
body, mind, and spirit. Intimacy happens in relationships as a
result of communicating on all three of these levels, psychologically and emotionally, nonverbally (including sexually), and

spiritually. While we will explore each of these areas individually, there is a synergistic quality of interweaving between each of them. In intimacy, as in a fine fabric, it is difficult at times to distinguish where one thread begins and another ends.

A very fine definition of intimacy in any close relationship is defined by Harriet Goldhor Lerner, in her *The Dance of Intimacy:*

Intimacy means that we can be who we are in a relationship, and allow the other person to do the same. "Being who we are" requires that we can talk openly about things that are important to us, that we can take a clear position on where we stand on important emotional issues, and that we clarify the limits of what is acceptable and tolerable to us in a relationship. "Allowing the other person to do the same" means that we can stay emotionally connected to that other party who thinks, feels, and believes differently, without needing to change, convince, or fix the other.

An intimate relationship is one in which neither party silences, sacrifices, or betrays the self and each party expresses strength and vulnerability, weakness and competence in a balanced way.[1]

We minister to hundreds of married people in our workshops and retreats each year and we have seen the tremendous joy as well as the pain midlife can bring. People whose lives have been surrounded by the sacramental bond of marriage and all of the related trappings of family, home, children, church, and commitment, which goes with it, walk into the midlife experience and can find their lives unexpectedly in chaos. Furthermore, due to the different times each spouse may experience midlife, couples need to understand the experience even before they enter it in order to deal with the turmoil their spouse may encounter. It is commonly understood that women enter into midlife at an earlier age than men.

TOM AND JEANETTE

Let us consider a couple in midlife and have a deeper look at their experience. Tom and Jeanette have just celebrated their Silver wedding anniversary. Tom is forty-five years old and Jeanette is forty-four. Their twenty-two-year-old son Steve has been away at college the past four years. Upon his graduation he rented an apartment with a few friends and lives in a nearby community.

He is engaged to a woman he met at school and they don't plan
to be married for a few more years. Among Tom and Jeanette's
concerns are that Steve and his fiancé may decide to live together
before their marriage. Their daughter Donna lives at home and
is attending a local state college in the evenings while she holds
a full-time position in a large pharmaceutical company. Donna
is twenty-four years old and finds it very comfortable living at
home. She has announced she has no plans to be on her own
until she has finished paying for her new car and has completed
some long anticipated foreign visits.

Tom is preoccupied with the heavy pressures of the small
company he manages. He believes his company has reached its
peak and often he works evenings and weekends to catch up
on his increasing backlog of work. He is concerned about several new firms in his field and he fears they will take much of
the business he has cultivated over the years. Tom's father lives
with them since a mild stroke several years ago. His medical
expenses are high and he does not seem to be getting any better.
Consideration of a nursing home has been a topic of conflict
recently between Tom and Jeanette. The financial strain of his
father plus the present and past college expenses has been distressing to Tom. He doesn't want to burden Jeanette with all of
this, so most of the time he keeps these concerns to himself.

While both are active and committed Christians, Jeanette
has been active in her local church for the past few years and
has a part-time job which began about six years ago when the
children were all finally in high school. She doesn't seem to enjoy
the job very much, but it keeps her busy and helps with the extra
expenses in the family. Both of Jeanette's parents are dead, yet at
times she still finds herself with a sense of loss over her mother's
more recent death. Jeanette does most of the cleaning and cooking in the household and most of her life and satisfaction have
been centered around her children and home. Unconsciously,
she fears her daughter will soon be leaving the nest so she tries to
do extra special things for her to keep her at home. She seems to
have adjusted well to Tom's father being with them, yet she feels
increasingly trapped between the job, children, and her failing
father-in-law.

When she thinks about the future, her options seem bleak
and limited. She questions her identity, what the future will hold

for her and her place in the world. Jeanette feels an inner emptiness and loneliness about her life. Something is not right, but she has a hard time defining exactly what is wrong. She resents her husband's long hours at work and sometimes feels like his job is more important to him than her. He doesn't seem to notice her pain and she finds herself unwilling to talk about it with him. She knows she wants more out of life, that she has a potential within that hasn't yet been tapped, yet she can't understand what happened to make her feel so unsettled. Her outer life hasn't really changed that much but inside she is in turmoil.

As a Christian woman she questions those inner stirrings. She thinks, "Should I really be experiencing all this uncertainty? Why can't I be thankful and grateful for the blessings I do have?"

Tom and Jeanette have always felt good about their marriage. They have attended church and been involved in the church community off and on. Most of their conversations seem to revolve around the children and Tom's dad and their concerns and responsibilities about them. There is little communication about themselves personally regarding their own pain or hopes for the future. Their marriage has become dull and routine for them both. Sex was good in the early years but it has become increasingly rushed and less satisfying. Tom and Jeanette feel constrained with the demands with which they are confronted: letting go of the children, the pressures of job and aging parents, the questioning of this inner turmoil, and facing what is happening in their own relationship.

Jeanette and Tom are each experiencing a midlife transition in a different manner. Both are feeling the grief of their loss and a questioning of present identity and self-esteem. Each one's inner crisis is enhanced by the other's pain and by the quiet breakdown in their relationship. If midlife is an invitation to intimacy, what can Tom and Jeanette do to deal with their individual lives and their relationship with one another to draw them into a deeper intimacy with themselves, one another, and God?

COMMUNICATING EMOTIONS

Just as for Jeanette and Tom, midlife brings with it new demands and questions for all of us. Where one or both have reached the point of midlife, it is essential for couples to communicate about what is going on inside of them. It is likely that Jeanette and Tom don't comprehend completely what these unsettled feelings and stirrings are all about themselves and may hesitate to verbalize them to anyone including each other. This is especially true if intimate communication has not been developed and nurtured earlier in the marriage. Yet, if a couple is sharing, at a deep and intimate level, their newly evolved fears, anxieties, hopes and dreams, they can be of great support to one another.

With the arrival of midlife should we find ourselves and our relationship in the midst of crisis, how can we grow in intimacy and trust which is so very vital? What are the areas of confrontation with which we will be faced? Each of us likely has a situation different than do Tom and Jeanette, but perhaps there are some threads of similarity.

Transitions and changes at midlife have the potential to call us to a growth and newness of life we may not have otherwise experienced.

A woman in childbirth suffers, because her time has come; but when she has given birth to the child she forgets the suffering in her joy that a man has been born into the world. [John 16:21]

As we reflect upon and examine our life in the midst of this change, can we see our own patterns of growth which we sometimes see as foolish, as sharing the patterns and purpose of the life of Jesus Christ? Can we have a deep trust and belief that God is present and with us even amidst the difficult transition of midlife? Midlife is truly "Holy Ground," and the Lord does lead and guide us. We are not likely to experience God's presence in the same way as in the past but perhaps we are being prepared for a deeper and more intimate divine relationship. Remember, midlife is just that, an invitation to intimacy.

Let's look at those three levels of communicating intimacy in marriage — psychological, sexual, and spiritual — and explore each more deeply.

COMMUNICATING PSYCHOLOGICALLY

Intimacy of mind and psychological well-being involve communication of our thoughts, feelings, aspirations, values, and dreams. Our views and experience of midlife will likely be very different even between spouses, yet we need to trust one another enough to communicate about those conflicting ideas and areas. Vulnerability doesn't automatically happen; it takes a decision on our part to share the depths of who we are as persons with one another.

This is especially so at times when we are not certain ourselves of who we are. Vulnerability is risky but it can also be the path of growth and intimacy which we need in order to enter into the individuation process of the second half of life.

I, Carol Ann, find that many times it would be easier not to communicate with Bob on a deep level. I don't always find it easy or natural. Yet at this time of midlife I have a strong inner conviction that will not allow me to remain silent as I might have in the past. I believe it is God's grace working with my own psyche that calls me to this inner conviction. There are times I don't understand what is happening inside me, those times of uncertainty and questioning and doubt about myself and my attitudes. If I don't understand them, how will Bob? Especially at moments like these I try to make myself vulnerable and communicate those inner contradictions to him. The result is usually a clearer understanding and perception for us both. Fr. John Powell faces the issues of communication in his excellent book *The Secret of Staying in Love*.[2]

Tom and Jeanette are experiencing typical questions and changes in their lives, and these changes affect their perception of themselves. Tom's questioning of his career and the financial pressures can only build up if not shared. Who better to share with than Jeanette? Jeanette also can grow if she is willing to impart some of the new stirrings within her to Tom. It is at this critical time of life that the promises made at the marriage altar become most fruitful.

Listening to one another's pain is easier said than done. Listening is not a passive act. It involves being attentive to the speaker's feelings, body language, and the tone of his or her voice, not just the words said. To listen actively involves clarifying what we believe is being said by other persons, restating what they have said to check the meaning and to show that we understand. When we are truly listening to one another, we are not called to have all the answers, nor to solve our spouse's problems, nor to correct one another, but to simply listen, care, and understand.

SELF-ACCEPTANCE

The level of psychological intimacy of a couple will depend on the individual foundation of how well each knows himself or herself. This self-intimacy is an important aspect of midlife growth and a vital expression of the marriage relationship. My awareness and love of myself play an important role in our relationship as a couple. As we mature we are asked to befriend ourselves. To be more cognizant of our strengths as well as limitations. Self-acceptance means to like oneself at this age and stage of our life. This allows us to live in the present more fully and so to avoid a denial of who we are at this stage in our life cycle. As we grow in our own self-understanding, the resultant confidence in ourselves allows us to be more vulnerable and open to our partner. We may also be more accepting of the other's weaknesses as we come face to face with our own shortcomings. You can only love another as much as you love yourself.

ESCAPING MIDLIFE

There are dangerous escape routes in midlife. One way of not facing the pain and unlived potential in ourselves is to deny that a crisis exists and to blame others for our problems. Another is work addiction. This can take the form of keeping ourselves constantly busy at work, making ourselves believe we are indispensable.

For myself, Bob, I continue to fall into this trap. I often find myself constantly in motion in an effort to stay busy. I have realized there are several reasons for this *busy-ness*. For one thing, I was taught the American work ethic very early in life. I was constantly told that I had to stay busy. As a youngster, when I had a productive job, whether it was picking apples, delivering papers, or mowing lawns, I was affirmed as good. Like so many hard-working Americans, I began to assume that my value was found in what I *did*. Not to say that this ethic is wrong, but it took me a long time to realize that who I am is just as important, if not more important, than what I do. I still fall into this trap, but I am working on it. Another reason I am prone to this behavior is my unconscious fear of the quiet. What will I experience if I slow down? What if nothing is there? It is only in my practice of *being* that I begin to trust that I can slow down and be at peace with myself. I often need Carol Ann's help to remind me of this need.

For a woman this same phenomenon can take the form of getting a job to escape her emerging self. We might need to ask ourselves if we are really developing our talents and gifts in our new career. Does our career choice help us to use our untapped potential as a woman of God or are we escaping a feeling of boredom and emptiness and do we need the affirmation of a paycheck? We must remember that meaning and affirmation in our life come from finding our true identity, using our potential, and recognizing we are sons and daughters of God. Only we can discern what is right for our life. If a job or career can help us to accomplish the individuation process at midlife and still maintain a balanced life, it may be the right choice for us. We will discuss appropriate and inappropriate midlife decisions further in chapter 12.

Excessive drinking, compulsive eating, and sexual affairs can be other attempts to avoid the midlife transition. These attempts to equivocate the pain of midlife may work for a time, but the "piper must be paid." One day the consequences of our avoidance will present themselves. We will discuss this consequence further in our final chapter.

MIDLIFE CONFLICT

In *Marrying Well*, James and Evelyn Whitehead examine many areas of concern at midlife. One area is conflict.

Conflict is normal in interpersonal exchange, it is an expectable event in the intimate lifestyle of marriage. Whenever people come together in an ongoing way, especially if significant issues are involved, we can expect that they will become aware of differences that exist between them. Sometimes these differences will be simply noted as interesting. But often they will involve disagreements, misunderstanding and discord. It is here that the experience of conflict begins.[3]

If handled properly, conflict can be a constructive midlife event. Conflict can show us areas of discrepancy between us.

You may think your oldest child should be disciplined one way and your spouse has a different idea. One spouse may be anticipating the freedom of an empty nest and would like to move to a smaller home and to pursue a simpler lifestyle, while the other partner wants to use new-found financial freedom to buy a more spacious home of which they've dreamed for many years. Other areas such as job, money, privacy, and sex are a few of the key areas that may come in conflict at midlife. Are we willing to explore the discrepancies in our differing views, needs, and ideals so we may come to know one another more fully? Growing in mutual respect for one another, especially when our ideas are different, can be a tremendous opportunity for growth as a couple.

RELATIONSHIP CYCLES

Dr. John J. Sherwood offers a wonderful model of relationships that can be of value when understanding midlife conflict. The model is valid for nearly any sort of relationship, be it between business associates, friends, children, or with an institution such as church, but it is particularly valuable when looking at our marriage. He maintains that relationships begin with a period of romance during which there is a free sharing of information and negotiating expectations. While we are greatly simplifying the model, this period is followed by a period of stability and productivity. After time, there often comes a disruption which he calls a "pinch" (minor disruption), or "crunch" (major disruption.) Participants in the relationship can deal with these disruptions via a "planned renegotiation" for the pinch (the most healthy process) or if a crunch, through a period of anxiety and uncertainty. In this latter process three alternative resolutions can occur. First, the relationship can simply terminate. Second, there can be an unsuccessful negotiation in which things return to the way things used to be, and finally, the most productive outcome will be a renegotiation which culminates with new sharing of information and negotiating expectations.

During this renegotiation, we decide what has changed. Marriage partners may ask if one of our needs changed or has one of us changed the way we meet the other's needs? While this is naturally the key step for the continuity of the relationship, it can only come about with a nonjudgmental attitude and understanding that needs can and must change especially at midlife. When the relationship is approached from this understanding, we can move out of the destructive cycle of blaming one another or taking on responsibility for the other's pain and discomfort. When we accept the premise that change is inevitable, we can begin to embrace the change and discover the new ways by which we will meet these changes. Change is painful and we often enter this stage defensively and with anger.

Undoubtedly there will be issues to face and conflict may result, which may be handled either constructively or destructively. Conflict is handled destructively when we become defensive and attack on a personal level, accusing the other of being at fault. This will likely generate very strong emotions. We can begin name calling and bring up old issues of hurt between us. To avoid this, it can be extremely helpful in opening such communications to use only "I" messages ("I feel lonely when..."), which concretely express my own viewpoint and feelings without blaming the other ("You make me feel...").

As mentioned above, one of the most common occurrences leading to and prolonging unresolved conflict lies in the area of taking responsibility for the other's struggles. In other words, if our spouse seems remote, or displeased, or angry, it must be because of something I did. When we approach conflict with the resultant sense of guilt or defensiveness, our communications are likely to be greatly distorted. I, Bob, remember the tremendous sense of freedom that came one day in the realization that I was not responsible for Carol Ann's moods, irritations, and emotional lows and anger. This realization was akin to a *conversion* experience. This issue is often referred to as *ownership of problem*. In other words, if Carol Ann seems out of sorts tonight, whose problem is it? When I take responsibility for her mood, I take ownership of her problem. Then the "problem" becomes something for me to solve or fix. In reality, her mood is just that, her mood. I cannot be present to the true nature of her problem when I approach her with the attitude that her resultant mood or feelings are my problem.

We have learned through years of practice that our moods or irritations often do not have a root cause in someone's action or violation of the other. Often they come from some unconscious source. If our spouses approach us with the idea that they have

to fix our problem, they cannot be what we truly need; someone to *listen* to us! During the pain of liminality and midlife
in general, most assuredly there will be times when we do not
understand ourselves and will need, more than anything else
in the world, one who will help us to understand these newly
discovered uncertainties and concerns. A spouse who can listen without feeling responsible or threatened will be the most
important asset we have.

Conflict is a difficult topic for most couples and one that
many couples do their best to avoid, but it can bring us a deeper
intimacy with one another. It can strengthen our marriage and
help us to look at areas we need to face in our evolving midlife
relationship.

Finally, comments on midlife conflict would be incomplete
without mentioning the painful reality of irreconcilable relationships. While the changes of midlife are painful, there is occasionally a relationship that must be terminated. For some, this truth
has existed for many years and only the maturity brought forth
by midlife can reveal the destruction which can go on by continuing an unhealthy and even psychotic relationship. Such a
decision should quite naturally be made only after much prayer
and counsel.

SEXUAL INTIMACY

This is why a man leaves his father and mother, and becomes attached
to his wife; and the two become one flesh. They are no longer two,
therefore, but one flesh. So then, what God has united, human beings
must not divide. [Matthew 19:5–6]

An area of great importance at midlife and all through married life is sexual intimacy. Many couples agree that the intimacy
of their sexual relationship increases significantly at midlife. The
younger years of marriage may have been very good, but nothing compared to the fine wine that has been aged and ripened
over the years. Bob and I spent our twenty-fifth anniversary at
a honeymoon spot in the Pocono Mountains of Pennsylvania,
one of those places seemingly reserved just for honeymooners.
Fireplace, swimming pool, whirlpool, all in view of the round
mirrored bed! We were there for three days and enjoyed every
glorious minute of it. We took our time and, knowing much bet-

ter how to please one another than we did twenty-five years ago, we made our original honeymoon seem a mere warm up.

With the maturity of midlife, other-centeredness looms larger in our sexual relationship, and we may be more free to respond fully to new levels of sexual fulfillment. The midlife years have a significant effect on our sexual relationship for a number of reasons. First, as discussed in the previous chapter, our own latent contrasexual nature is beginning to surface, and this can call us to different and often interesting roles in all parts of our relationship, including our sexual alliance. A man's evolving feminine nature may allow him new freedom in the marriage bed as he allows himself to take on a more playful, passive, and receiving role. Likewise, a woman's developing Animus may provide her with a newly discovered ability to take the sexual initiative and play a more dominant role. Further, with children grown and fears about unwanted pregnancy diminishing, we are afforded an increased opportunity for freer sexual expression.

Sex as Communications

But most importantly, with the often inexplicable shifting emotions of midlife, we need to avail ourselves of every form of communication possible to convey our mutual love, concern, and intimacy to avoid the breakdown so common in today's world. The invitation to intimacy with another in midlife is lived out for married people in the intimacy of their marriage. Physical and emotional intimacy culminates in their marriage bed.

Any significant unresolved hurts, frustrations, and resentments between a couple will eventually affect the flow of sexual feeling between them. This is one reason why honest communication is essential to nip any unresolved feelings in the bud before they have time to fester. When a couple is struggling in any other area of their relationship, whether it be about finances, the children, their career, changing roles and values, it will affect their sex life.

Sexual intimacy may often help reconcile the pain which partners cause one another. There are times when words fail and nothing seems to bridge the gap between two individuals who are strongly at odds with one another. Their nonverbal yet powerful sexual communication may remind the couple they are one and may help heal the wounds of life. Sex is not a substitute for verbal communication but, when practiced in conjunction with one another, the two weave together beautifully as one.

COMMUNICATIONS ABOUT SEX

As always, but especially at midlife, it is helpful when a couple is explicit and specific about what they like or dislike in sex. While our needs, interests, and desires may or may not change at midlife, our thirst to discuss our needs is never greater. Even if we have negotiated into the patterns we now use, it may be time for a serious dialogue to clarify our current ideas. Indeed, this can be a part of our continuing pattern of midlife renegotiations.

We need to tell one another what gives us pleasure. How do we like to be touched and caressed? What causes the greatest sexual satisfaction for each of us? We should give ourselves time to once again experiment and leisurely enjoy one another's bodies. Carol Ann and I will occasionally go out to dinner to a quiet and intimate place with the expressed agenda of talking about what we each enjoy in bed. Such a night makes for a beautiful, fun evening that culminates in the crescendo of our marriage bed.

All of this contributes to a healthy and ever more enjoyable sexual relationship. The intimacy and caring we have for one another in all the areas of our relationship can be heightened as an essential key to helping one another through this time of midlife transition. The Sacrament of Matrimony calls us to a profound sharing of ourselves on all levels, the emotional, the prayerful and the physical.

In *The Freedom of Sexual Love*, Joseph and Lois Bird offer, in straightforward language, an extremely helpful view of sexual intimacy in the Christian context. They try to explode some of the old sexual myths and taboos that many of us carry and they replace them with a beautiful concept of sacramental married sex.[4]

SPIRITUAL INTIMACY

A growing measure of spiritual intimacy in the life of a couple can see them through many trials and difficulties. There is a strong connection between our sexual and spiritual intimacy. In the gift of our Sacrament of Matrimony we are called to be a sign to the world of Christ's love and presence. We are called as a couple to live out our spirituality in our marriage relationship. Thomas L. Vandenberg writes in *A Companion for the Pastoral: A Sign for our Time:*

Through the unity of love expressed by the sexual desire between a husband and wife, God is letting us in on the profound desire He has to be one with us, a unity Our father wants for all His people with one another, in His son, Jesus (Jn. 17:21). With this understanding, the sexual desire of husband and wife for one another must be seen as both spiritual and sacramental.... Sexual desire is at the very heart of the couple's spirituality as a couple. It cannot be separated from their way of life. It is at the very core of their way of life. This means, obviously, we are not limiting our attention to genital activity between husband and wife. On the contrary, it is an attitude of mind and heart that permeates every aspect of the couple's relationship.[5]

Our individual relationship with the Lord will also affect our relationship as a couple. As we are attuned to hear and respond to Jesus in our own prayer time, we will in turn bring the grace of that response to our marriage relationship as we live out that response to Jesus in a concrete everyday way.

PRAYING TOGETHER

Praying together as a couple can be a difficult step for many. We may feel prayer is too private, just between ourselves and God. At midlife, if we are responding to our call to intimacy with God and with one another, a natural step can be to become more vulnerable and begin praying with one another. Praying together is as individual and varied as there are married couples. The intimate experience of coming together in prayer may take the form of reading and reflection upon scripture together. It may take the form of praying the rosary or spontaneous prayers of petition, laying our needs at this time of life before God. At midlife there are often many issues churning within us, some of which we don't agree upon. As together we bring these issues before God, his grace is at work in allowing us to let go of the control that is often no longer appropriate at midlife.

An example of this may be praying for our children daily, not necessarily for specific changes, but that they may respond to God in their life and in their relationships with others. We can pray together asking for God's wisdom in making our parental decisions involving discipline, schools, clarifying values, and the many issues involved in raising children in this age. As our adult children leave the nest and go out into the world, we have less influence on their decisions and lifestyle. Our prayers can help us to let go and at the same time allow us to place them more and more in God's care.

We may decide to pray together before we make decisions that affect our future, such as a job or career change. We may pray individually or as a couple for our spouse and the struggles they are experiencing at midlife. We may decide to celebrate daily Eucharist together. The gift and grace of the Eucharist may draw us closer as a couple and individually to the Trinity.

Bob and I pray the Liturgy of the Hours together in the morning and evening. This is a set of prayers using the Psalms and Gospels which is used universally within the Catholic Church. We sometimes vary the set routine with song, worship, and our personal prayers and petitions. Praying as a couple reinforces the power of Jesus in our everyday life situations. Praying together can help to open us to needs of others in our parish, community, and the world. This connects with the call to generativity which is a focal point of the second half of our life. We may pray about what we can do as a couple to make our world a better place for the next generation. Our prayer may call us to action on the level of social justice on a global or local level. Whatever the invitation, we may ask in prayer how we as a couple or as individuals can respond by using the talents and resourcefulness with which God has blessed us.

Our own experience of praying together as a couple has grown and changed throughout the years. Since our return to the Church in 1976, praying at meals has been an everyday part of our lives. Whether we are home or in restaurants, alone or with others, we try to join in grace together. We have found that after lovemaking is a natural time for thanking the Lord for the gift of one another and the intimacy we have just shared.

There have been moments in our relationship when I, Carol Ann, just needed to be embraced by Bob and held close or needed his affirmation. To me that has been a prayer, for surely God does surround me with love by using Bob's tenderness and warm, firm embrace. At midlife, when things are troubling us that we can't even verbalize to one another, often it is sufficient to feel the quiet and serenity of being still together before the Lord and allowing God's love to heal us and bring us to an inner peacefulness where we can be touched by the Spirit.

The natural flow of our intimacy as a couple should touch other people. What we have received we should freely give to others or our own love will become stagnant. What form of service can each of us as an individual or as a couple be involved in to allow the love we have to flow on to others?

11

Personality and the Midlife Transition

In our book *Personality and Spiritual Freedom*,[1] we attempted to provide a simplified, Christian approach to C. G. Jung's theory of Typology as measured and expanded by Isabel Briggs Myers, creator of the *Myers-Briggs Type Indicator*. For those unfamiliar with this very useful theory, a brief summary follows. After this brief explanation, we will offer ideas relative to type and the midlife experience.

FOUR PAIRS OF OPPOSITES

Essentially, Jung's theory of Typology, one of his earliest, describes four pairs of opposite personality characteristics: *introvert* and *extrovert*, *sensing* and *intuiting*, *thinking* and *feeling*, and finally *judging* and *perceiving*. Each of us instinctively prefers one of each of these pairs over its opposite thus giving us one of sixteen possible personality types.

INTROVERT AND EXTROVERT

One of the easiest to identify, the introvert and extrovert differ in their attitude and disposition toward the outer world. The introvert usually prefers the inner world and consequently is often more quiet and reserved. Introverts tend to process their information on the inside by *chewing* on it before making their decisions. They will often prefer fewer, more intimate relationships in their personal lives. The extrovert, on the other hand, prefers the outer world of people, places, and things. Extroverts like to be involved in life in an attempt to better understand the world. They tend to be more outgoing and assertive and they process information on the outside, sometimes saying things in an effort to understand them.

Energy

The most significant difference between introverts and extroverts is their source of energy. The extrovert is energized by the outer world. When involved with people, projects, and events, extroverts seem to get their batteries charged. While they certainly slow down and become quiet at times, a prolonged period of quiet and isolation can be draining to extroverts. They can become restless and impatient for action. Introverts, on the other hand are energized by the inner world. They need to slow down and come to their own quiet in an effort to charge their batteries. Given a long period of socializing or interacting with a large number of people, events, and projects introverts will likely wilt and need some quiet to regain steam.

Blends

In the introvert and extrovert pair of attitudes as in the pairs which follow, it is important to understand that no one is purely one type or the other. Each of us is a *blend* of both characteristics, yet we tend to prefer one over the other. We can use both our right and left hands to do certain tasks, but we naturally much prefer to use one hand over the other. Each of us can and does use both our introversion and extroversion daily, but, given no opportunity to choose our behavior, we will quite naturally use one or the other most often. This is known as our *preference*.

SENSING AND INTUITING

The sensing and intuiting pair of functions deals with how we *receive information* from the world. The person who prefers the sensing function is the detail-oriented person who receives information *serially*, one fact after another. They tend to live life based on their experiences and for this reason tend to dislike change. They can often recall great details from the past. The intuitive, on the other hand, receives information *intuitively*, that is, in parallel, one big bite after another. They tend to dislike details and would much prefer to think of whole concepts, leaving the details to others (usually sensors).

Time Dimension

One of the significant differences between these two is the time dimension they prefer. The intuitive prefers to live more in the *future* mode, preferring to think of the possibilities. Consequently, they are the idea people who have a propensity for discovering what *could be* rather than *what is*. The sensor's time dimension is the *present*. They have a gift of the here and now. They like to rely on past experience and what is tried and true. Again, recall that each of us is a blend of sensing and intuiting, yet we prefer one over the other.

THINKING AND FEELING

The thinking and feeling functions deal with how one *makes decisions*, how one *acts upon the world*. One who prefers the thinking function makes decisions using logic, facts, and their opinion of objective truth. They have a gift of organizing facts logically and they tend to be brief and businesslike. Rules, policies, and truth are much more important to the thinker than are circumstances and relationships. Conversely, those who prefer the feeling function elect to make their decisions based on harmony, relationships, and values. When they act upon the world, they will have more of a concern about specific circumstances and the feelings of those involved. Their disposition to relationships makes them much more attuned to harmony, and often this is the overriding factor in their decision making.

JUDGING AND PERCEIVING

The judging and perceiving attitudes deal with individuals' preferences for acting upon the world or having the world act upon them. This is true regardless of whether they prefer to make decisions using the judging functions of thinking and feeling or the perceiving functions of sensing and intuiting.

Those who prefer the judging attitude are those who like to reach closure on any options or projects before them. They much prefer to make decisions and get things finished than to have loose ends. Judgers tend to be organized and purposeful. They like to wrap things up and, when decisions are before them that they cannot close out, they are inclined to become anxious and tense.

The antithesis of the judger, the perceiver prefers to leave all options open and make sure all the information available on a subject has been gathered before something is settled. More in the *perceiving* mode, they allow life to come to them rather than feel a need to act upon it as their judging counterparts. As a result of their open disposition to the world, they tend to be quite spontaneous and may like surprises.

After considering these qualities in much more detail than here, through the use of the Myers-Briggs Type Indicator and a qualified consultant, people may decide for themselves their preferred personality type from each of the four pairs. As a result they determine their overall type such as an "introvert, intuiting, thinking, judger" or an "extroverted, sensing, feeling, perceiver," and so on. There is a Myers-Briggs shorthand that assigns letters to each of the characteristics:

Introvert = I
Extrovert = E
Intuiting = N
Sensing = S
Thinking = T
Feeling = F
Judging = J
Perceiving = P

Consequently, one's personality type can be identified as an INTJ or an ENFP, and so forth.

As we have discussed, while we have a naturally preferred set of personality characteristics described above, we are all blends. That is, we can and do use our least preferred characteristics, but with less spontaneity, skill, and confidence. In using our undeveloped functions and attitudes, for example, a feeling type making decisions using the thinker's logic, truth, and justice, perhaps we will do so in a clumsy manner, finding it difficult, sometimes feeling childish, awkward, and uncertain. This is much like using our left hand if we are right-handed and vice versa.

PERSONALITY AT MIDLIFE

In chapter 8, we spoke of the paradox of opposites emerging during the reintegration stage of midlife. Among the many opposites we will encounter during midlife will be the opposites described above. Midlife is a natural time when the unacknowledged aspects of our personality (those qualities that are not part of our type) call for our attention and recognition.

These undeveloped qualities in our personality are part of our shadow described in chapter 7. As a result of our development over the years, our ego builds its persona using the natural gifts of personality type. Thus thinkers develop a persona that uses logic, truth, and justice in a somewhat impersonal way. When temptations or circumstances arise which tempt them to use their feeling function's harmony, values, and relationship, they will often deny such behavior and relegate the experience to the confines of the shadow.

It is during midlife that this undeveloped shadow side of our personality needs to be more consciously integrated into our personality if we are to reach the wholeness and freedom that God seems to desire for us. Midlife is the time when we are called to reach a balance in our personality. If we are an introverted type, which means we are energized by solitude and calm, the inner world being our main arena, then at midlife we are called to develop and exercise more freely our extraverted behavior.

I, Carol Ann, am introverted and I am sometimes very energized, much to my surprise, after working with large numbers of people in our ministry. But I still find, after long periods of interacting with so many people, perhaps over a period of a few weeks, that I need to take some time alone again to be re-energized. Nevertheless, I find I desire a lot more interacting with others than I did during the first half of my life.

Bob, on the other hand, the extrovert, seems to need less interaction. An extrovert is energized by being involved with people and things and by being in the middle of the action. Here, the natural midlife call inward will invite the extrovert to slow down and begin to integrate the beauty of the quiet and meditative side of his or her personality. At midlife we can begin to consciously exercise our opposite preferences so that we do not remain too one-sided in our personality.

During midlife we may notice that our least developed function will give us the most trouble. This is the one that usually resides deepest in the unconscious and is the most difficult to integrate with our conscious, outward personality. As we become more aware of how these characteristics call for our attention, we will notice how easily we become bothered with them and how difficult it may be to integrate them.

For example, my (Carol Ann's) least developed function is sensing. When my work calls for gathering details, I often unconsciously rebel. For me, details are boring and tiresome. Recently, while doing research for this book, I found it frequently necessary to look in many sources for specific details. As this called forth the detail-oriented sensing function, my weakest, I was often inattentive. I would begin reading, become absorbed in the overall concept of the author (the gift of the intuitive), and read right past my sought after fine point!

FREEDOM

As a result of this material being a part of our shadow, it can affect the way we interact with and treat other people. We can and do project our inferior functions on other people. The sensor whose gifts lie in the details and the here and now, may find himself or herself infuriated by the future-oriented intuitive who is judged to be "spacey," to have his or her head in the clouds. Using our rule of thumb from chapter 4, if our emotional response to such people is out of proportion to the circumstances, we are likely projecting our shadow onto them. Likewise, we can find ourselves in custody of our shadow personality type when we are behaving in a very untypical manner. For example, this might happen when those who prefer intuiting find themselves obsessed with the details of a circumstance or project and cannot withdraw themselves. Here we are in the grip of our shadow.

As discussed in chapter 7, such behavior is destructive because, when we are projecting, we are not seeing the actual person upon whom we are projecting. Rather, we are seeing our own weaknesses in the mirror of another. Likewise, when in the custody of our shadow, we are not behaving in freedom.

To grow in freedom is to be able to call freely upon all eight personality characteristics, according to the circumstances, the Gospel values, and according to God's Will for us at the given time. This is a difficult and life-long journey, but one that needs to be especially considered at midlife.

PERSONALITY AND THE STAGES OF MIDLIFE

Given the stages of midlife, separation, liminality, and reintegration, and the characteristics of the second half of life, personality type can tell us something about our preconditioned disposition toward the entire midlife experience. How might we *do* midlife? Using our natural personality gifts, are we more likely to embrace the midlife experience or resist it?

Introvert and Extrovert at Midlife

As we look at the introvert and extrovert combination, we notice that the introvert is more comfortable in the inner world. Recall that the midlife experience and the entire second half of life are a call inward to better understand who we are and how we are made. Moreover, the second half of life carries with it a deeper call to God and carries with it an implicit need to listen to God more fervently in the quiet. In responding to these calls, we are in the natural realm of the introvert. Extroverts will likely be most comfortable with the outward focus of the first half of life. When they hit midlife, they are likely to find it more painful to make this transition from their preferred world to this somewhat foreign firmament of the inner world.

Sensing and Intuitive at Midlife

Intuitives may find the future orientation of midlife a bit more to their liking than the here and now sensate. They may be able to look beyond the pain and discomfort of the present midlife transition and see the potential which lies in the second half of life. The intuitive has the gift to be able to see a myriad of possibilities even in adversity. Our own experience is that it is usually the intuitives who will have the most positive attitude during the midlife transition. Sensors prefer to live by their experience. What has worked in the past should work in the future. This adage simply doesn't hold for the midlife experience, and the sensing type may indeed struggle with this incongruity.

Putting to use the new and untried is not one of the sensor's natural gifts.

Thinker and Feeler at Midlife

The thinker who wants life to be orderly, logical, and just, may well struggle with the lack of logic and order that midlife customarily brings. Midlife is anything but logical and orderly, although, for me, Bob, who is a thinker, looking at it with the structure presented throughout this book has given the process an order I had not expected to find in the chaos of midlife. The inability of thinkers to get a grasp on their ordinarily controlled emotional life can be terrifying to them as well. Conversely, feelers who may be much more attuned to listening to the feelings of themselves and those around them, may find the challenge of midlife a more endurable experience. Their natural preference for harmony may be of help or hindrance during midlife when their projections come more alive and they are increasingly irritated by others. Yet feelers may put this preference to use as they attempt to move closer to God in responding to the natural call of the second half of life.

Judger and Perceiver at Midlife

This final pair of attitudes is probably the most relevant to the three stages of the midlife transition as the tension between reaching closure and leaving options open comes into play. Perceivers who prefer to leave their options open may be willing to experience midlife in a much deeper way than their judging counterparts. Their aversion to reaching decisions helps them hold onto the prime task of the core element of the transition. That is, the task of liminality to simply *embrace the liminality*. This can only be accomplished by remaining in the experience, being willing to hold off reaching closure until the full value and grace of the in-betweenness has been absorbed. However, the reluctance of perceivers to reach closure may render them unwilling to make the move into the new nature of the second half of life when their experience of liminality has reached its conclusion. By the same token, the judger, wishing to move on and bring the somewhat painful uncertainty of the midlife experience to a conclusion may be so anxious for closure that the judger fails to accomplish this vital task of liminality.

While this theory gives us much to contemplate in our own personality makeup and the midlife transition, it is only food for thought and not meant to be interpreted rigidly. Most people experiencing transition have numerous ups and downs. Change is not easy for us, no matter what our personality type. Although understanding the theory can be a valuable insight and understanding ourselves from this perspective can help us respond to the midlife call to grow in intimacy with ourselves.

As we have only been able to scratch the surface of the fascinating subject of personality types, we recommend that those who find this approach to personality and midlife helpful obtain a copy of our previous book, *Personality and Spiritual Freedom*, or any of a number of fine works on the subject.

12

Discernment

As we pointed out in the Introduction, we live in a society which does all in its power to avoid pain. Indeed, this is natural and the pain of liminality is no exception. The lack of any seeming *productivity* during much of midlife and of liminality in particular causes us to fight the process and do all we can to quickly move through it.

FALSE STARTS

The most frequent and natural reaction to the pain and uncertainty of the liminality of midlife is to make changes in our lives. In fact, making changes is necessary to test the waters of our unfolding future. Changes can take many forms, some minor and some major. Perhaps we will begin to exercise or stop smoking in an effort to treat ourselves better. We may change our diet. Some people join health clubs and weight loss programs.

We may want to change a routine or pattern of behavior. Perhaps our prayer life will need a tune up or we will vary the place where we go to church. Often people in midlife begin to attend retreats or prayer meetings or Bible studies.

Some of the changes are symbolic. While my full name is Carol Ann, for most of my life I went by the name Carol and that seemed to be fine for me. When I was in my late thirties, I attended a retreat and was praying and reflecting on my personal history. I recalled both of my grandmothers and how I remembered them being very close to God. They had a profound influence on me in many ways. I recalled that my full given name was in honor of both of these women. When I returned from my retreat, I decided that I would like to be called by that full name once again. Bob and some of my friends were somewhat surprised, and it took a while for everyone to get used to it. My name has much more meaning for me today and now stands as a symbol for a much deeper significance in my life.

Our changes may be as simple as a new hair style or a new color of suit. Or perhaps a new way of relating to someone in our life. Perhaps we try a new method of interacting with someone. Possibly a parent, a child or an in-law. Some of these trial changes will be appropriate and some will not. On the natural level some will seem to fit and others will be uncomfortable, and we know we will have to continue looking.

I, Bob, recall during my career with the Bell System attending management training courses where the instructors invited the participants to "try on" new ways of relating to other people or of expressing ourselves. We were assured no feedback would go to our superiors and we were in a "safe" environment to try out new personality techniques. While my usual "style" was to be up front and aggressive, I occasionally took those opportunities to chance a more "laid-back" disposition. It was always an interesting experience and we occasionally invite participants in our retreats to do the same thing.

During midlife we might look into other types of possible variations on our behavior. While we might join a new club, take a class, or try a new hobby, we might also venture some new purchases. No industry seems to understand the psychology of midlife better than the automobile industry. Many of us can walk down our block and count the midlife cars which fill our neighborhood garages. (Perhaps one of them is our own!)

All of these attempted changes can be natural responses to the liminality of midlife. Each is part of the process of discovering our new identity and the process is indeed necessary.

The task of discernment at midlife is to determine whether our proposed changes are really appropriate to our personality, lifestyle, and state of life. We will try something out to see how it works and how it fits, much like trying on a new pair of shoes.

Yet we must be cautious. Not all of our responses to midlife are appropriate. We will be constantly tempted to make changes which are not *creative ways* of dealing with change but desperate attempts to avoid the pain and discomfort midlife changes often bring. Indeed, we all know of those who have had an affair as part of their attempts to avoid the pain of midlife. The incidences of infidelity and divorce during the midlife years are sad testimony to the way our society deals with troublesome change.

Dramatic job changes and relocations may be ideal responses to the change of midlife, but they too can be inappropriate and disabling responses. My own brother (Bob's) will quickly attest that his decision to resign as the general manager of a manufacturing firm and buy a New England resort candy store was not appropriate for him and his family. Yet, at the time of the move, it had all the markings of a positive creative response. (We're convinced resort-area real estate brokers make their living selling midlife dreams.)

We may also know of men or women who have set out to acquire their long-dreamed-of undergraduate degree or advanced degree and still others who have entered the ministry at midlife. In our own church (Roman Catholic) many men have become permanent deacons as a result of a midlife call. For some this change is fitting and for others it is not.

For ourselves, at ages forty and forty-one, we decided Bob would resign from a high-paying job, we would sell a beautiful home, and begin a totally new lifestyle. Today, six years later, the decision seems to have been appropriate. Yet others have made similar decisions and the decision proved to be unsuitable.

DIFFERENTIATING APPROPRIATE FROM INAPPROPRIATE MIDLIFE CHANGES

How do we discern if a major midlife move is appropriate or not? As we have said, what is appropriate for one may well be inappropriate for another. While we are not able to offer a concrete set of ideas which will successfully identify what is or is not a befitting midlife decision, we will offer some thoughts.

Our frame of reference will be our list of the characteristics of the first half of life versus the second half of life introduced in chapter 2.

STAGES OF LIFE

First Half of Life	Second Half of Life
Outward Focus	Inward Focus
Establish Identity	Striving to Balance
Career Choices	Spiritual and Personal Growth
State and Style of Life Choices	Discover Value of Crosses
Intimacy with Others —	Forgiveness of Self and
Family, Community, etc.	Others
Conquer the World	Authentic Identity
Sunrise Perspective	Sunset Perspective

By looking at these two lists as well as the list of the characteristics of the three stages of midlife, we can begin to understand a sense of what may be suitable midlife decisions. One of the most important, but not *the* most important question we must ask ourselves about our midlife decisions is, "Will this change move me closer to features of the first or second half of life?"

To consciously discern our decisions we need to understand the intensely different focus of life to which we are moved during midlife. The second half of life carries with it a more *inward focus*. We are called to move toward a more authentic identity as Child of God. Will the changes we are planning draw us toward the inward focus of the second half characterized by the discovery of our authentic identity or toward the outward focus of the first half? Are we still trying to *make our mark in the world* in accordance with our sunrise mentality or are we moving toward a mission for our life which comes from a better understanding of God's Will for us? Are we still trying to make career choices that will give us an outward identity to replace the one we built in the first half which now seems hollow?

ROLE AND IDENTITY

Major midlife decisions are often muddled because they involve both our role and our identity. When persons make a career change or enter the ministry or acquire a new degree, they take on a new role in life. In addition, they often take on the identity of their new career or title. Thus career and educational changes are often decisions which involve not only what we do but also who we are and how others see us. Frequently the combined elements of role and identity are present in the decisions of our middle years.

AN EXAMPLE

In our ministry and among our friends are many considering entering the permanent deaconate in the Catholic Church during their midlife years. For those unfamiliar with that role in the Church, a commitment to enter the deaconate involves three to four years of intensive training, full cooperation of the man's wife, family, and pastor, and a life-long commitment to the local bishop as well as celibacy should he enter the deaconate single or become single through death of his spouse. The role of deacon is one of ministry. They receive the Sacrament of Holy Orders the same as a priest but without certain faculties such as the ability to consecrate the Eucharist or absolve sins. Often they have the opportunity to preach at Sunday Mass, minister the Sacraments of Baptism and Marriage, and a host of other ministries open to the larger Church.

Needless to say, the decision to become a permanent deacon is a major, irrevocable decision and one which is often made during the midlife experience. Midlife ministry decisions can be among the most difficult to discern because they involve a healthy amount of inner energy from the second half of life as well as a large dose of ego identity, the focus of the first half. Yet all would agree the decision should be made primarily because it is precipitated by a call from God.

Using this decision to enter the deaconate as an example, what process might one use and what questions might one ask to help determine if such a decision was appropriate in one's middle years? In this decision, as in all midlife decisions, one of the primary questions to ask oneself is "*Why?* Why do I want to do this? What is my motivation? What am I trying to accomplish with this new role and identity?"

Looking deeply into our motivations is not an easy task, yet, on its very own, doing so is a task of midlife. We need to search the reasons why we want to do things to discover if the call to which I am responding is an outward call or an inward call. In other words, am I more concerned with the role and identity which others will perceive me to be once this decision is implemented or can I exclude that outward role as a part of my decision? If no one were to ever know that I will take on this new role, would I still pursue it?

Certainly all of us are affected by the outside world as none of us live in a vacuum. Yet how much are we affected by the world's opinion of us in this decision?

As so much of our motivation is unconscious, it can be difficult to really touch on our underlying motives. We may be able to understand a little more of our need for others' approval of our new role by looking at our own perception of others already in our targeted role. How do we look at others who now serve as deacon or whatever role it is we are moving toward? What is my attitude toward them? Am I awed or envious? Do I daydream about how it would feel to be in their place? Did my attitude toward and relationship with others now in that role *change* once they had made their change into the new role?

MOVING TOWARD SECOND HALF?

We can look at the characteristics of the second half of life and try to determine if our motivations are related to an authentic movement toward those more fruitful concepts. Am I responding to a need for a more inward focus of my life? Will this new role help me to function out of a more authentic identity? Will it represent a response to God's call for me, and who *he* desires me to be? In this new role, do I sense that I will be more of the Child of God I believe God wants of me?

As we answer these questions, we are deeply involved in the answer to the entire dilemma: *discernment*. Discernment is achieved only through prayer, introspection, and listening. We need to detach ourselves from the temptations of the world. We must listen with an open heart.

To aid in the discernment process, a retreat can be extremely valuable. Over the period of a week or longer one can enter into what is known as a "silent directed retreat." In such a retreat, we enter an atmosphere of prayer and silence which can afford the opportunity and quality time to quiet down and truly listen to God speaking to us. During a directed retreat we meet with a spiritual director once or twice a day. The balance of the day would be spent in periods of prayer, exercise, and reflection. The Spiritual Exercises of St. Ignatius is a thirty-day extended silent retreat for the purpose of discernment in one's life. If such a length of time is impractical, the retreat can also be made at home over a period of months with regular meetings with a director. Taking such quality time is valuable as we make major life choices and decisions.

It is our hope that the questions we have raised in this chapter will help our readers in this key task of midlife: discernment of the will of God for us.

13

Healing at Midlife

I have been crucified with Christ and I no longer live, but Christ lives in me.
—Galatians 2:20

If we understand midlife as a wonderful time of grace and truly an invitation to intimacy, there are many things that we can do to cooperate with the process. We need to do our own part and not expect God to do it all for us. His grace and our response work together. We need to see this invitation to intimacy with God as valid for ourselves no matter how far we seem to be from God or how close to him we believe ourselves to be. Complacency means the demise of growth.

Now more than ever, our life of prayer needs to be nurtured and reinforced with a sense of regularity and a listening heart. Listening to the inner stirring of the Spirit and responding with a discerning heart can move us toward healing and unforeseen joy and growth at midlife. It is a time in our life to truly "let go and let God."

Healing at midlife is not something to be rushed. When we are in the pain of a crisis, it is difficult to allow God to heal our lives slowly and gradually. We would much rather have it be quick, easy, and painless. Yet if we progress patiently and unhurried as we move through this time of healing at midlife, we won't have to return again and again to reopen old wounds. If we are experiencing a difficult time in a specific area of our lives, it may be impossible to feel God's presence, but by faith we know he is with us. It is sometimes only when we have passed through the storm that we can look back and recognize that Jesus was there all the time.

PRAYER

A significant part of the healing process at midlife should include prayer. Where are you in your relationship with Jesus in prayer? Do you have a regular prayer routine? What scriptures most touch your heart or stir your innermost being? What type of prayer draws you closest to the Lord? Wherever you are in prayer, there is always more.

Contemplative prayer can be very fruitful at midlife. By contemplative prayer we are referring to prayer requiring little or no words. In this type of prayer you are in God's presence and there is an intensification of loving openness. Prayer of the quiet may be difficult for some because we are used to doing all of the talking in prayer. The second half of life requires more listening and simply "being" with the Father, Son, and Holy Spirit. We need to use prayer that helps us get in touch with Christ who dwells within us.

The Jesus Prayer

The Jesus prayer can touch the depths of our unconscious. Slowly repeating the name of Jesus, first verbally then silently. Allow the name of Jesus to fill your body, mind, and spirit, to flow to your entire being. Allow yourself time and quiet space to move into this type of prayer. You may spend long periods of time completely quiet. Contemplate short verses or even just a few words from a scripture and allow those words to speak to your heart. In these types of prayer we aren't necessarily looking for any answers or profound insights. If they come to us, that is an added grace. If not, this kind of quiet prayer alone can help us come to that desired second-half-of-life stance of open hands, depending more on God and being receptive to the Spirit in our life.

The closer we get to the Lord, the more we realize the Father, Son, and Holy Spirit are intimately involved in all of our lives. Not just our time of prayer, but every aspect of our day and in all of our relationships. Being faithful to prayer helps us to become more attuned to this reality. There is nothing in our life that God does not want to be involved with.

Prayer of the Body

We may also be drawn to different types of prayer, such as using our body in movement and gesture. The Psalms are very conducive to this method of prayer. We could take a few verses of a psalm or a scripture and put gesture with the words as our prayer to God. This involves our whole body and allows it to become actively involved in our worship and prayer. Christian music can also be a resource that we can use for dance or gesture in prayer. This type of prayer may seem to be more feminine in nature but can be very valuable and freeing for men at midlife as a way to touch the feminine within their unconscious.

I, Bob, was surprised that such a prayer would work for me. During a retreat, I was invited to follow some prayerful music with my body and discovered a very freeing form of prayer. I believe the attraction had much to do with the emerging midlife feminine side of me.

Art as Prayer

We may venture to use clay or art in our prayer. This can be done in many varied ways. You may use the scripture Jeremiah 18:5–6:

Then the word of the Lord came to me: "O house of Israel, can I not do with you as this potter does?" declares the Lord. "Like clay in the hand of the potter, so are you in my hand."

With your eyes closed take the clay in your hands and feel its texture and explore the feeling of the clay. Sense its warmth or coolness, see how it feels as you begin to work it with your hands. As you are doing this, allow the words of the scripture to come back to your mind. Form the clay in any manner you would like and take your time with the process.

After another time of prayer, you may want to form a symbol with the clay representative of your time with the Lord or where you are in your relationship at this point. Use your imagination for the variety of ways that clay may be helpful for you in prayer. These forms of prayer may touch aspects of your unconscious that could tell you much about your relationship with God.

Similarly, another form of prayer may be drawing. There is no need to have previous experience. All you need are some crayons, pastels, or watercolor. Take a large piece of paper and draw a circle on it. The circle is a symbol of wholeness and represents an aspect of who you are right now in your life. Have the colors before you and choose what appeals to you at the moment. You may want to begin with a scripture or a reflection on how you feel about yourself or your relationship with Jesus. You may reflect on a specific area of change at this time of midlife or a feeling you are experiencing which you don't understand. You may choose a relationship in your life that is joyful or troubling to you. Take some quiet time to reflect before you begin. Also, ask Jesus to lead and guide you in this process. As you begin, choose the colors that suit your mood or how you are feeling. There is no need to draw anything specific, just designs or colors or shapes of any kind will do. Take your time with this process and be mindful that it is a reverenced time of prayer. This type of art is known as a mandala.

When you are finished, write somewhere on the paper how you felt when you were drawing. It may be helpful to date the drawing. Stand back and look at the picture, maybe even turning it at different angles. Keep it some place prominent where you can view it frequently. See how the colors or symbols speak to you. See if it relates to anything in your life at the present or something you are experiencing. If you have a spiritual director, share it with him or her. If not, show it to a close friend or your spouse and talk about how you felt creating it and also anything that might have struck you afterward. If you find this type of art a helpful addition to your prayer, you may want to save these drawings as part of your journal.

JOURNALING

Journaling can be especially valuable to use for our prayer and inner work. After a time of prayer or of reading scripture it is helpful to record in your journal what you heard in your time of prayer. You may also want to record thoughts and feelings as you read or reflect on scriptures. You may want to write a letter to Jesus about how you are handling this time of midlife or a specific area of concern for you.

It is very helpful to date what you record in your journal for further reference when you go back to read it. You will eventually find, after keeping a journal, that there may be a certain pattern or rhythm to your spiritual path. It may be helpful to look back to times of difficulty to see how the Lord has dealt with you in the past and what helped you to feel God's love and grace at moments of darkness and pain. Recording the consolations you have received and moments of intimacy with Jesus may be valuable to you not only at present but also at a time when things aren't going well. You may want to record some of the major happenings in your outer life to see how they correspond to what is occurring inwardly or vice versa.

A journal can be a helpful tool in recording our dreams of and dialogues with those unknown aspects of ourselves that are coming to light. Prayer is an effective vehicle for getting in touch with those hidden parts of ourselves that seem to demand our attention during the middle years. It is through a listening heart that we hear the inner stirrings of our shadow and the contrasexual qualities found in our Anima or Animus.

PRAYING WITH OTHERS

Praying with your spouse or a close companion can be valuable anytime in your life, but especially at midlife when there may be much uncertainty and ambiguity within us. Having a partner who is praying with you and for you can give that added strength and support needed at this time. Intimacy with God and another may be increased and nurtured through praying with another.

GROWING IN SELF-KNOWLEDGE
THROUGH PRAYER

Midlife is a stirring that *invites* us. An invitation by its nature is a luring, a bidding. God never imposes growth on us, nor violates our free will. Thus, as we will see in more detail in the final chapter, it is we who decide to go on this journey or not.

Self-knowledge and prayer go hand in hand. The awareness we gain about how God has made us is beneficial and even crucial at midlife and on our spiritual journey. At the core of our being, where Christ resides, we find the deepest desire of our heart and thus God's Will for us. These insights are not readily accessible to us through our ego but can only be found in prayer as we come in touch with our true identity as son and daughter of God the Father. Prayer can open the flow of communication between the ego and God's Will, between the conscious and the unconscious. When there is a natural flow of communication between the ego and God's Will for us, we are better equipped to make the best and most selfless choices for our life. By nature our ego alone would seem to have all the right answers, but the objective is to have the ego function with the benefit of God's Will for us, found at our center. Ultimately as the bridge between our ego and God's Will is built, we will be making choices more in freedom and in accord with God's plan for our lives.

When I look into the eyes of Jesus, who does he say that I am? What is my true identity as Child of God? There are many forms of false ego identity that may need to be removed if we are to find the way to our true self. We focused upon this in earlier chapters. My role, occupations, accomplishments, relationships, possessions, talents, and appearance are a part of who I am and are a gift of God, but if we solely relate to those or find all our worth in them, we are surely missing our central focus. My authentic identity may be found by reflecting on some of these scriptures.

You are God's work of art, created in Christ Jesus.

[Ephesians 2:10]

Do not be afraid, for I have redeemed you, I have called you by name, you are mine.   [Isaiah 43:1]

Thus says Yahweh, your redeemer, he who formed you in the womb.

[Isaiah 44:24]

I have loved you with an everlasting love, so I am constant in my affection for you.   [Jeremiah 31:3]

Ask God to reveal to you your true worth and identity through His eyes. Ask God to reveal these things to you in your time of prayer and in your life circumstances. In midlife, as we grow in deeper understanding of our true identity from God's perspective, it will assist in numerous other areas of our lives.

In St. Teresa of Avila's writings on prayer she speaks often

of the importance of self-knowledge and the link it has with
her relationship with God. She compares her journey in prayer
with the symbol of an interior castle. There are many rooms
in the castle and each is a step in growth in our prayer and
relationship with God. The center room is where Christ dwells.
As we journey, we know ourselves and our intimacy with God
go hand in hand. The individual is a pilgrim who is journeying
to a place where the human and divine meet.

RETREATS

Retreats are another path of healing in midlife. It is important
that we be convinced of God's interest in our healing. A retreat
gives God a chance to communicate in a special way at a special
time and place. There are retreats specifically on midlife. We
have had the blessing of leading many such retreats. These may
give you opportunities to specifically pinpoint and pray about
areas in your life where Jesus is calling you to change and grow.
It can also be beneficial to know that the things we encounter in
midlife transition are experienced by other Christians. It can be
comforting to know that some of these difficulties are a normal
part of growth in the midlife years and that they can be ways of
calling us from death to new life and wholeness.

There are numerous retreats offered on areas of understanding and processing the inner journey, retreats such as those focus-
ing on dreams and spiritual growth. Some retreats focus on the
healing of memories and these can be especially beneficial in the
area of forgiveness of ourselves, others, or even God. The theme
of forgiveness is important in midlife healing. There are other
retreats concentrating on journaling, dealing with our anger and
guilt or retreats specifically for couples. There are also varied
weekends on different forms of prayer, maybe some that would
be new to us. We have had the blessing of leading many retreats
with a variety of formats throughout many parts of the world
and we have seen how valuable they can be to participants.

Other retreats that can be fruitful at midlife are silent or
directed retreats about which we spoke earlier. During this type
of experience there would be no formal talks or input sessions.
Rather, most of your time would be spent praying and reflecting
on scripture or aspects of your relationship with God. You may
meet with a director for a short time each day to talk about how

God is being revealed to you, and the director may have some prayer suggestions for you. It is amazing to us when we are in an atmosphere of quiet, away from our everyday routines, how clearly we can begin to hear the voice of God speaking in our life in a variety of ways. These quiet retreats can last for a weekend or a week, or even for extended periods of time. They can be times of knowing God's love and grace in our lives that we carry with us throughout our entire life journey.

Other areas of healing in midlife are doing just what you are doing in reading this book: learning about yourself and what you and your loved ones are going through. You may want to be a part of a midlife group in your parish where you can come together to pray over and share topics relevant to your journey.

Other tools for healing at midlife are recording your dreams, praying about them, and realizing their deeper meaning for you in your life. Further help in working with dreams was presented in chapter 12.

SPIRITUAL DIRECTOR OR FRIEND

Having a spiritual director or a companion to share our inner journey will be as valuable at midlife as at any other time. It can be important to have a person with whom we can be completely honest and with whom we can share the pains and joys of our life and our relationship to others and God. This kind of relationship takes trust and vulnerability. Reflecting, verbalizing, and sharing our journey with another gives us ownership and authority. It is one thing to be aware of our story; verbalizing it can make it even more concrete and real for us. As we keep a spiritual journal, we may want to read parts of it with our spiritual director.

As we grow in our prayer and relationship with the Lord at midlife, the area of spiritual discernment is important. To be able to discern between the Holy Spirit, the evil spirit, and our own human spirit in areas of our life is an important insight toward which to grow. At midlife when we may be experiencing some difficult and painful interior movements, it can be most beneficial to understand where they are coming from. When we are in desolation and feel that God is very distant or when we are doubting ourselves, sharing this with another is part of the way we can deal with these interior movements.

At midlife understanding and dealing with areas of the shadow can be brought into prayer and shared with a spiritual director to help us integrate and deal with these facets of ourselves. A spiritual director or someone who has training in depth psychology and the midlife transition and who is also a person of prayer would be a wise choice.

Many diocesan offices have names of qualified spiritual directors or retreat houses to contact which have directors on their staffs. You may meet with a few before you find the right person for you.

PROFESSIONAL COUNSELING

During the transition of midlife, counseling can be extremely beneficial. This is especially true at such a major transition with the potential for healing and lasting change. We may find ourselves hesitant and questioning about seeking professional help because many of us carry a very negative idea about such help. We were taught psychiatrists were only for "crazy people." One who went to such professionals were considered weak and unstable. This attitude is unfortunate and it prevents many people who could greatly benefit from counseling from seeking such help.

Today a variety of counseling professionals are available to us who can work hand in hand with our physician and our spiritual director. Here we see the value of treating the whole person, body, mind, and spirit. Counselors are today available through many social organizations including churches. Most diocesan offices are able to refer parishioners to qualified counselors if they do not have them on their own staffs.

There are many reasons for not wanting to go for counseling. In our workshops we've heard them all: "It costs too much." "I don't have any way to get there." "I don't know where to find one." "I can work my own problems out." "I had a friend who went once, and it didn't help." "It's not me who should go, its my husband, and he won't go." In John's Gospel, Jesus asks the cripple at the pool of Bethzatha, "Do you want to be well?" This is the question we too must ask ourselves when we are invited to seek professional help. Might not all of our excuses be our way of avoiding healing? Might we not be more afraid of getting well than staying as we are? If we were to get well, might we lose our excuse for our irrational behavior today?

Professional counseling works with God's grace. If we seek help and continue with a life of prayer and many of the other recommendations given earlier, God can and will use the human sciences to bring us to the healing he desires for us.

Relative to professionals, we offer one caution for Christians. It is important that we seek Christian counselors or those who are comfortable with the Christian experience. All too often, counselors are hostile to the religious experience because this is what many psychological theories teach. Seek recommendations from other Christians who have successfully used counselors and don't be afraid to ask a counselor his or her opinion of the Christian experience. This includes counselors attached to church ministries as well.

FORGIVENESS AND HEALING

Penance, the Sacrament of Reconciliation, and fasting are all meaningful and pertinent choices to help us in our transitions of midlife. Forgiveness is a major area of growth as we move to the second half of life.

Areas may come to our attention that we have not dealt with during the first half of our life that may require healing and forgiveness. Wanting to be honest before our loving Father and with another, we may find God's healing touch moving us to love and accept ourselves and others.

The Sacrament of Reconciliation encountered on an ongoing basis can assist us in recognizing and accepting our sinfulness as well as God's grace and love as we grow through the transitions and changes of midlife. Living with the ambiguity of saint and sinner takes an openness and honesty with ourselves and with God.

In this age where everything is so readily available to us, fasting and penance may be difficult for many, but the grace that flows from these acts is pertinent to our spiritual growth. Do we hunger and thirst not only for outer nourishment but also for that inner food and drink, that fulfillment only our God can provide?

PLAY

The need to allow the inner child to have some space in our life is essential at midlife. We can do this by finding ways of play and recreation which, because of our busy lives, we have put aside and sometimes even consider frivolous. We can ask ourselves if there is something we can do just for ourselves, something we would really enjoy. It may be a hobby or sport, to learn a new language or study a new area of interest. Whatever it may be, taking time to do things that are lighthearted and creative can help restore balance to the one-sidedness of our life.

In their book *Mid-life Directions*,[1] Sisters Janice Brewi and Anne Brennan say that our prayer and playing make our living more God-like. These two areas are central experiences of midlife. There may be a connection with our willingness to enter into enjoyment and pleasure at midlife and our capacity for enjoyment and pleasure in eternal life. How can we love and enjoy God in the next world if we cannot love and enjoy God in this world?

An attitude of play is also important for couples in their relationship. Are we willing to take time to be lighthearted with one another? It is so easy to get caught up in all the important things in which we are involved, but the area of playfulness can help give us the balance we need in our relationship at a time when there are some very difficult areas with which we must deal. Our attitude in life and our ability to laugh and be lighthearted can even affect our physical health. Negative emotions produce negative chemical reactions in our body and positive emotions produce positive chemical reactions in our body. What are our attitude and thoughts on being more playful?

Finding an enjoyable routine of physical exercise has proven helpful for many. A daily routine of walking, biking, swimming, or whatever, can effect you not only physically but emotionally and spiritually as well.

THE HEALING TOOLS WORKING TOGETHER

My own (Carol Ann's) experience of transition at midlife was helped by many of these instruments of God's healing and love. I was very blessed to have a spiritual director who was conversant with the midlife process and depth psychology, and also a person of deep faith. During this time I experienced much anxiety and inner turmoil which I found very disturbing. I didn't understand what was happening to me or really how to channel the energy in a positive direction. I began keeping a journal of my dreams and also of the strong feelings I was experiencing during those days. It helped very much to write them down to make them more concrete for myself. I began seeing some patterns in my feelings and anxiety that were surprising to me. I was also spending time in prayer and reading scripture. When I felt overwhelmed by stress or pain I would do Mandala drawings, using watercolor or crayons. I would choose a color that I was drawn to and make shapes or designs. When I was finished, I would write the feelings I was experiencing as I was doing the drawing. All of these things were discussed and discerned with my spiritual director. Between the tools with which I was working and meeting with my director for over a year and a half, I began to come to a point of inner healing. I see now how that time of transition and crisis was a turning point for me knowing myself and Jesus much more intimately. It took several years to integrate all that was happening and for the wounds of my transition to be healed.

As I look back now I can see things much more clearly. My spiritual director was there and was an active listener. He allowed me to share the depth of my pain and uncertainty without judging me or giving me answers. It was a time for me to recognize my pain and to be with it. Not pushing it out of sight or tucking it away, but allowing the pain to have space in my life. It was difficult but now I see how fruitful it was for my whole spiritual process.

During this same time I was taking some college classes. I was learning things that really excited me. It was a new venture for me and I found a lot of untapped energy in myself. I also began a daily physical routine of exercise. I found that it helped with my stress and had a very healing effect on my body as well as my emotions and spirit.

My husband, Bob, was very supportive. He was always there just to listen to me share my pain and hurt. He was there with an acceptance of me just as I was in all my brokenness. He didn't try to solve my problems or give me answers, but he listened with his heart. There were times when I just needed to be embraced and the freedom to cry in his arms. He was there for me. I see now how important all of these things were in my time of midlife transition. The transition ultimately brought me into a deeper intimacy with myself, God, and my spouse.

The things I learned at this time in my life are still an important part of my journey today. I am through this one aspect of midlife but I know I still have to walk through other doors ahead. God is faithful. His love and mercy are even more real for me today.

My prayer for you at this time of midlife is that you may find a companion or spiritual director that is knowledgeable in the process of midlife, one who will listen to you and love you. Someone who will call you to be all God desires you to be in the second half of your life. With God's grace, love, and mercy you too may be thankful for your suffering and pain that may lead you from death to the resurrection and new life in Christ Jesus our Lord. It is in our weakness that Christ can be our strength.

QUESTION FOR PERSONAL REFLECTION
AND SMALL-GROUP SHARING

Suggested Scripture: Ephesians 3:16–19

Out of his infinite glory, may he give you the power through his Spirit for your hidden self to grow strong, so that Christ may live in your hearts through faith, and then, planted in love and built on love, you will with all the saints have strength to grasp the breadth and the length, the height and the depth; until, knowing the love of Christ, which is beyond all knowledge, you are filled with the utter fullness of God.

PERSONAL PRAYER AND REFLECTION
PRELIMINARY NOTE

You come before your loving God who desires to bring you to wholeness and healing. Allow the divine, infinite love and acceptance to touch your very depths.

1. *Ask Jesus to be Lord of your deepest self and to reveal to you your true identity in relationship with the Father, Son, and Holy Spirit.*
    Reflect upon the following scriptures, what do you see as your true identity as Child of God?

We are God's work of art created in Christ Jesus.
[Ephesians 2:10]

I have loved you with an everlasting love, so I am constant in my affection for you.
[Jeremiah 31:3]

Do not be afraid, for I have redeemed you; I have called you by name, you are mine.
[Isaiah 43:1]

2. *Midlife is an opportunity for spiritual growth. With God's grace and love and our willingness, we can find the new life Jesus desires for us.*
    Bring before the Lord your heartfelt need at this time of your life. Allow Jesus to speak to you about that need.

3. *God often speaks the divine will to us by planting it as desires deep within the core of our being. In a time of deep reverence and prayer, try to discover the deepest desire of your heart and allow Jesus to speak to you about that desire.*

SMALL-GROUP-SHARING QUESTIONS

1. *When do you feel closest to Jesus? Do you find it easy or difficult to be still with God? Describe your present style of prayer. Have you noticed changes in recent years?*

2. *Of all the areas of healing at midlife, which are you most drawn to explore more deeply? Why?*

3. *Do you have a close friend or spiritual director to talk with about your relationship with God as well as this time of midlife transition? Would you find this helpful? Elaborate.*

4. *Do you allow time in your life to be playful? Describe. Do you do something that brings you enjoyment such as music, art, hobbies, and so on? How do you feel about play and recreation in your life? Have you noticed a change? Are you willing to add more play to your life?*

14

The Invitation

I am offering you life or death, blessing or curse. Choose life, then, so that you and your descendents may live.
—*Deuteronomy 30:19*

This final chapter is one of caution and hope. It is one of caution because, as we have made clear throughout this work, midlife comes upon us as an invitation. An invitation is not a mandate. An invitation implies a choice and choice always conveys freedom. We are required to *choose* to make the successful midlife journey. The fact is, *we don't have to make this journey!*

Of course midlife will come upon us whether we like it or not. The choice we have to make is whether to deal creatively with the changes brought about by this transition and thus to make it a time of opportunity, growth, and blessing or to fight it.

FAILURE AT MIDLIFE

And we can fight it. Millions do. To fail at midlife is an all too common experience. In fact, some of the estimates of the number of us who make a successful midlife transition, compared to those who fail at midlife, are dismaying. Some estimates run as high as a 90 percent failure rate. As you can see, many choose not to make the journey.

To fight the transition at midlife is to invite tragedy and failure. It is the forerunner of our forfeiture of the beauty of the second half of our lives which seems to be God's plan for us.

What does it mean to fail at midlife? To fail at midlife is such a common experience that nearly all of us can quickly identify people who have not made a successful midlife transition. When people fail at midlife, they choose not to move on to the gifts and qualities of the second half of life but to revert to the traits of the first half of life with a more relentless and rigid attitude than they held during their earlier years.

For example, the business person who fails at midlife is, at age sixty, much more driven, goal oriented and harsh than he or she was at thirty. Such a person can become a workaholic with no relationship with family and with none of the mellowness that should come with later years.

Another example is the mother who fails at midlife. She becomes the compulsive mother-in-law or grandmother who cannot let go of her children or is always looking for someone to mother or more likely, "smother." She is often unable to move into new interests and more appropriate relationships using her latent gifts and qualities.

There are many examples of our failure to deal properly with midlife. Always, they revert to the characteristics of life's first half.

INTIMACY

Scripture is filled with texts on the core call of midlife: *intimacy.* The entire theme of the book of Hosea is a call to come back to God wholeheartedly. Jesus says,

Come to me all you who labour and are overburdened, and I will give you rest. Shoulder my yoke and learn from me, for I am gentle and humble in heart, and you will find rest for your souls. [Matthew 11:28, 29]

The entire book of the Song of Songs deals beautifully and symbolically with the issue of intimacy.

Intimacy with God comes to us in many ways. We can be intimate in moments of prayer and meditation. We can be intimate as we come to know better the person of Jesus in the scriptures. We can grow in intimacy as we allow God to rule our lives more and more by discerning the divine will for us.

In addition, *to be intimate with ourselves is to be intimate with God.* Intimacy with ourselves means to really discover the person God wants us to be: to seek out the gifts with which he has endowed us; to seek out the personality he has chosen for us; to seek out the mission he desires for us. Indeed, our God has planted all of this truth within us, at the deepest part of our being, within the Self, God's Will for us. With grace we can come to know this will.

But this sort of intimacy involves a deep and sometimes frightening vulnerability. This vulnerability involves a letting go. Letting go of all I, in my ego-oriented, outward focus of the first half of life, thought I was for these past forty years. Letting go of the persona or mask or identity I have striven to build for the benefit of others: my role as mother, scientist, executive, teacher, mechanic, priest, religious, minister, and so on. Vulnerability may involve a letting go of all I have built, my possessions, my "things," my children, my relationships. To become vulnerable as I let go of the *dream* I have built for those same forty years so it can be reevaluated and perhaps redrawn in a new light.

Jesus said, "If you wish to be perfect, go and sell your possessions and give the money to the poor and you will have treasure in heaven; then come, follow me." But when the young man heard these words he went away sad, for he was a man of great wealth. [Matthew 19:21, 22]

Do we really want to make this journey?

Indeed this often painful letting go involves a death. A dying to ourselves, and it is painful. But *we choose whether to go.*

BROKENNESS

This vulnerability comes only as I place myself before God with open hands and humility. As we do this, we make the step toward intimacy which is the call of midlife, and the first painful discovery we may make is our own brokenness. We often come face to face with the reality that after forty or fifty years we still don't have it all together. With all of our possessions, titles, and accomplishments we are still lost. We discover that under this veneer there stands a terrified little boy or little girl who shivers and wants to cry when things don't seem to go our way. We may discover our loneliness and distrust about people and life and perhaps even God. We confront these discoveries only in humility and vulnerability. Is it any wonder that we fight the process? But, *we don't have to make this journey.*

To confront this lonely darkness can be what St. John of the Cross called the "dark night of the soul," and it involves confronting our poverty of spirit. This is what conversion is built upon: humility. Can we recall again why Jung, in his many years of practice as a therapist, could make the statement that he never saw anyone healed who did not get in touch with his or her God? One could not confront this sort of poverty without the grace of God nor the comfort of knowing one was loved by God. It is too easy to run away, and in our increasingly secular society many choose not to make this journey.

PASCAL MYSTERY

During the midlife journey we enter, perhaps more than any other time in our lives, the Pascal mystery of Christ. We find ourselves walking through the archetypal passion, death, and resurrection first fully walked by Jesus.

If experienced well, we will feel the pain of the passion as we enter the separation stage of midlife with it's letting go of the past and grieving over our losses. As we experience the death of liminality, we enter Christ's "in-betweenness" when he was neither alive in heaven nor on earth. Perhaps we, too, feel the darkness of our own tomb during this painful time. Finally, we can experience the full joy and promise of the resurrection as we advance into our life's second half in the reintegration stage. Here is the promise. As Christians, just as we walk through this life with faith in the assurance of the resurrection, we can walk through the uncertainty of midlife with faith that we, too, will experience the exhilaration of the new life.

We in the Church have frequently failed to provide the spiritual connection for our people at midlife. We have not offered them the spiritual and psychological encouragement needed to make this journey. Indeed, we find our own ministry is so rewarding because of the joy people express when this frightening journey is explained, and they are "authorized" to experience some of the trauma the midlife transition brings with it. The midlife transition is far too spiritual for the Church not to provide the guidance its people need.

Ignatius of Loyola experienced and thus taught that we truly discover God's Will by becoming detached. By purging ourselves to the point that we can pray in earnest, "Take, Lord, receive all I have and possess.... Your love and your grace are enough for me."[1] He had his followers spend thirty days in prayer, silence, and fasting to bring themselves to the point that they could hear God's Will by detaching themselves from their physical and emotional possessions.

DO WE REALLY WANT TO MAKE THE JOURNEY?

But do we really want to know God's Will? When Jesus met the cripple at the pool of Bethzatha, he asked, "Do you want to be well?" Do *we* want to be well? Do we want to be whole? Will we allow ourselves to become old? In a society that idolizes youth, can we see the beauty of becoming older?

Do we really want to take this religious journey seriously? The midlife excursion is a deeply spiritual journey. It is a safari into the unknown. Jesus spoke to us when he said to Peter:

In all truth I tell you, when you were young you put on your own belt and walked where you liked; but when you grow old you will stretch out your hands, and somebody else will put a belt round you and take you where you would rather not go. [John 21:18]

Will we allow *others*, the others within us, our unconscious others, our hidden "zoo," to take us where we would much rather not go? Can we be willing to listen to the message of our shadow, our Anima or Animus, our inner child, the Christ within?

What is the deepest desire of our heart? What truly is God's Will for us? Can we let go of all else to follow this? Can we let go of all else to follow new and uncharted waters in the hands of our inner guide: Jesus the Nazarean? Can we trust ourselves enough to believe that what we want at the core of who we are, God also wants for us? Will we leave all else to follow this?

NOT WITHOUT RISK

While it is not the focus of this book to expand upon the concept of evil and original sin, it is well to advise caution when we delve deeply into God's Will for us. In our search, we may well find more than we are looking for and the task of discernment becomes crucial. While we believe God's Will does reside at our core, it is surrounded by unconscious energy which can lead us astray. Within our repressed and hidden *junk* we can find evil which may make itself appear as God's Will. The presence of the Evil One is real and his ability to use the secret confines of our depth is legendary. Within us is a wonderful potential for good, yet the potential for evil exists as well. The concept of original sin bares witness to humanity's ability to tap into the evil that seems to "hang around" the good within us. "I am offering you life or death, blessing or curse. Choose life" (Deuteronomy 30:19).

So, we come to the end and we come to the beginning. Each of us must make a choice when we enter midlife. For some it is a conscious choice; others allow their unconscious to make the choice for them. Will we make the journey or not? Indeed, we have made it clear that *we don't have to go*, yet we hope those who have shared these pages will choose to go, will choose to make what can be the most exciting and fulfilling journey of their life. Yes, the journey has its risks. Life has its risks. But the choice we make will determine the quality of the rest of our lives. We have only come half way. Often we stumble through the first half of life. The choice we are given here is to either stumble through the second half as well or to choose life: to choose to make the second half a time of fulfillment, blessings, and freedom.

Notes

Introduction

1. Robert and Carol Ann Faucett, *Personality and Spiritual Freedom* (New York: Image/Doubleday, 1987).

2. To contact the authors write to the publishers or Look Beyond Ministries, Inc., 228 Sky View Terrace, Effort, PA 18330.

Chapter 1: The Rhythm of Midlife

1. Robert and Carol Ann Faucett, *Midlife, Invitation to Intimacy*, six-part video series (Boston: Daughters of St. Paul, 1989; available from authors at Look Beyond Ministries, 228 Sky View Terrace, Effort, PA 18330).

Chapter 2: Stages of Life

1. C. G. Jung, *Stages of Life, Structure and Dynamics of the Psyche, Collected Works*, vol. 8 (Princeton: Princeton University Press, 1960), p. 5.

2. Ibid., p. 12.

Chapter 3: Stages of Midlife Transition

1. Murray Stein, *In MidLife* (Dallas: Spring Publications, 1983).

Chapter 4: A View of the Mountain

1. Fritz Kunkel, *Selected Writings*, ed. John A. Sanford (Ramsey, NJ: Paulist Press, 1984).

Chapter 5: Separation and Endings

1. John Welch, *Spiritual Pilgrims* (Ramsey, NJ: Paulist Press, 1982), p. 93.

2. Murray Stein, *In MidLife* (Dallas: Spring Publications, 1983), p. 28.

3. Dennis and Matthew Linn, S.J., *Healing Life's Hurts* (Ramsey, NJ: Paulist Press, 1978).

4. Elisabeth Kübler-Ross, *On Death and Dying* (New York: Macmillan, 1969).

5. See no. 3 above.

6. Harriet Goldhor Lerner, *The Dance of Anger* (New York: Harper & Row, 1985).

Chapter 6: Betwixt and Between

1. Marion Woodman, *The Pregnant Virgin* (Toronto: Inner City Books, 1985), p. 14.

Chapter 7: Liminality and the Shadow

1. Louis M. Savary, Patricia H. Berne, and Strephon Kaplan Williams, *Dreams and Spiritual Growth* (Ramsey, NJ: Paulist Press, 1984).

2. Robert Johnson, *Inner Work* (San Francisco: Harper & Row, 1986).

3. Robert Johnson, *We, Understanding the Psychology of Romantic Love* (New York: Harper & Row, 1983).

4. Ann Belford Ulanov, *The Feminine in Jungian Psychology and in Christian Theology* (Evanston, IL: Northwestern University Press, 1971), p. 29.

Chapter 8: Reintegration and Midlife

1. John Powell, *Happiness Is an Inside Job* (Allen, TX.: Tabor Publishing, 1989).

2. John Bradshaw, *Bradshaw on: The Family* (Deerfield Beach, FL.: Health Communications Inc., 1988).

3. Dennis and Matthew Linn, S.J., *Healing Life's Hurts* (Ramsey, NJ: Paulist Press, 1978).

4. Teresa of Avila, *The Collected Works of St. Teresa of Avila*, vol. 2 (Washington, DC: ICS Publications, 1980).

Chapter 9: The Other Man and Woman at Midlife

1. Tad and Noreen Guzie, *About Men and Women* (New York: Paulist Press, 1986).

2. Toni Wolff, *Structural Forms of the Feminine Psyche* (Zurich: Jung Institute, 1956).

3. John A. Sanford, *The Invisible Partners* (New York: Paulist Press, 1980).

4. Ibid, p. 59.

5. Robert Johnson, *He, the Psychology of the Masculine* (King of Prussia, PA: Religious Publishing Co., 1974).

6. Robert Johnson, *She, the Psychology of the Feminine* (King of Prussia, PA: Religious Publishing Co., 1976).

Chapter 10: Enriching Marriage at Midlife

1. Harriet Goldhor Lerner, *The Dance of Intimacy* (New York: Harper & Row, 1989), p. 3.

2. John Powell, *The Secret of Staying in Love* (Allen, TX: Tabor Publishing, 1974).

3. James D. and Evelyn Eaton Whitehead, *Marrying Well* (New York: Image / Doubleday, 1983).

4. Joseph and Lois Bird, *The Freedom of Sexual Love* (Garden City, NY: Doubleday / Image, 1970).

5. Thomas L. Vandenberg, *A Companion for the Pastoral: A Sign for our Time* (Elizabeth, NJ: Pastoral and Matrimonial Renewal Center, 1982), pp. 5–6.

Chapter 11: Personality and the Midlife Transition

1. Robert and Carol Ann Faucett, *Personality and Spiritual Freedom* (New York, Image / Doubleday, 1987).

Chapter 13: Healing at Midlife

1. Janice Brewi and Anne Brennan, *Mid-life Directions* (New York: Paulist Press, 1985).

Chapter 14: The Invitation

1. Ignatius of Loyola, *Spiritual Exercises*, Number 234 (St. Louis: The Institute of Jesuit Sources, 1980).